THE GOSPEL ACCORDING TO MARK

The Gospel According to

MARK

*With Notes
by Craig Munro*

JOHN RITCHIE LTD
CHRISTIAN PUBLICATIONS

40 Beansburn, Kilmarnock, Scotland

ISBN-13: 978 1 910513 59 0

Copyright © 2016 by John Ritchie Ltd.
40 Beansburn, Kilmarnock, Scotland

www.ritchiechristianmedia.co.uk

Printed with kind permission from Challenger Publishing

Typeset by John Ritchie Ltd., Kilmarnock
Printed by CCB, Glasgow

Contents

The Gospel According to Mark

This book, as the first verse states, presents the "gospel of Jesus Christ, the Son of God". 'Gospel' means good news and there are four gospel accounts of the life of Christ in the Bible. The Bible itself is an amazing book. It is actually a library of sixty-six books written originally in three languages, on three continents and over a period of 1500 years, by kings, commoners, priests and prisoners. Amazingly the message of each book is consistent with the whole. They tell us of the greatness of God and His desire to bless mankind. We hope that after reading one of the books of the Bible you will want to read them all.

The four gospels together provide a very full picture of the person and work of the Lord Jesus Christ. They are, however, not carbon copies of each other. Matthew the converted tax collector tends to concentrate on proving to a Jewish audience that Christ was the Messiah, the Son of David, the true King. Doctor Luke emphasises to a Gentile audience the perfect, holy, loving manhood of Christ. John, the fisherman, tells us explicitly that he writes his gospel in order that the reader might believe that Jesus is the Son of God and through believing in Him may obtain eternal life. Mark, on the other hand, seems to set out to prove that the Lord Jesus Christ was God's perfect Servant. This is why he starts at the commencement of the Lord's public service and tells us nothing of His early days in Nazareth. The gospel of Mark is punctuated with little words like "and", "immediately" (anon), "forthwith" etc. The reader races from one event to the next. It is emphasising the tireless energy that the Lord Jesus exerted in His full and perfect service down here on earth. Of course the climax to His service on earth was the cross of Calvary. There He would lay down His life voluntarily for the world. He, the sinless One, died for the sin of the world. He rose again victoriously and is alive to save all those who will call upon Him. This booklet is published with the prayer that you might receive Jesus Christ as your Lord and Saviour.

MARGINAL NOTES

This Gospel is published with marginal notes for three reasons:

(1) This translation is the King James Version, first published in 1611. Some words not in current use, or that have changed their meaning, need to be explained.
(2) There are themes or thoughts which appear throughout the gospel. Marginal comments allow the reader to trace some of these themes, and then re-examine the context and setting of each reference.
(3) Some biblical illustrations are not automatically understandable to a modern western mind and require explanation. Marginal comments of this nature are not frequent as we believe Scripture should speak for itself.

"Who then can be saved?"

Mark 10.26

THE *MEANING* OF THE WORD "SAVED"

This word "saved" is used many times in the Bible. It most commonly has the meaning of being rescued from sin, a purposeless life, or from God's wrath. Salvation is at the centre of God's intentions for mankind. The Name Jesus means Jehovah the Saviour. The angel said "Thou shalt call His Name JESUS: for He shall save His people from their sins" (Matthew 1.21).

EVERYONE CAN BE SAVED

The Bible states, "God ... will have *all* men to be saved, and to come unto the knowledge of the truth" 1 Timothy 2.3-4. The love of God extends to everyone without exception. "For God so loved the world, that He gave His only begotten Son, that *whosoever* believeth in Him should not perish, but have everlasting Life" John 3.16. The Lord Jesus died on the cross as "a ransom for *all*" 1 Timothy 2.6. *All can* go to heaven through faith in the Lord Jesus. Sadly not everyone will go to heaven because they have refused to accept God's love and His free gift of eternal life.

WE *CANNOT SAVE* OURSELVES

The disciples in desperation to know how they could be saved from God's wrath and enter the kingdom of heaven asked the question "Who then can be saved?" Mark 10.26. The Lord Jesus had just stated that it was easier for a camel to go through the eye of a needle than for a rich man to enter the kingdom of heaven! The Lord answered the bewildered disciples by saying, "With men it is impossible, but not with God". In other words, salvation is all of God. It is impossible for anyone to merit eternal life, no matter how good they are. Equally, no one is too sinful to be saved. God can and will save anyone who is prepared to acknowledge their sinfulness and accept His Son as Saviour. "By grace are ye *saved through faith; and that not of yourselves: it is the gift of God: not of works*, lest any man should boast" Ephesians 2.8,9.

WE *MUST BE* SAVED

Peter preached on the streets of Jerusalem "Neither is there salvation in any other: for there is none other Name ... whereby we *must* be saved" Acts 4.12. Please observe that the word is 'must' and not 'should' or 'might'. This is because there is too much at stake. To miss the gift of eternal life, the salvation of your soul, sins forgiven, a relationship with God through the Lord Jesus, is to miss everything and be eternally lost.

WHAT MUST I DO TO BE SAVED?

This is the most important question you can ask yourself. It is you that will have to face God for your sin if you refuse His offer of mercy. This question was asked by a jailor in Philippi when he keenly felt his own sin before God. The answer to such a question has never changed, "Believe on the Lord Jesus Christ, and thou shalt be saved" Acts 16.31.

Mark 1

1 The beginning of the gospel of Jesus Christ, the Son of God;

2 As it is written in the prophets, Behold, I send my messenger before thy face, which shall prepare thy way before thee.

3 The voice of one crying in the wilderness, Prepare ye the way of the Lord, make his paths straight.

4 John did baptize in the wilderness, and preach the baptism of repentance for the remission of sins.

5 And there went out unto him all the land of Judaea, and they of Jerusalem, and were all baptized of him in the river of Jordan, confessing their sins.

6 And John was clothed with camel's hair, and with a girdle of a skin about his loins; and he did eat locusts and wild honey;

7 And preached, saying, There cometh one mightier than I after me, the latchet of whose shoes I am not worthy to stoop down and unloose.

8 I indeed have baptized you with water: but he shall baptize you with the Holy Ghost.

9 And it came to pass in those days, that Jesus came from Nazareth of Galilee, and was baptized of John in Jordan.

10 And straightway coming up out of the water, he saw the heavens opened, and the Spirit like a dove descending upon him:

11 And there came a voice from heaven, saying, Thou art my beloved Son, in whom I am well pleased.

12 And immediately the spirit driveth him into the wilderness.

13 And he was there in the wilderness forty days, tempted of Satan; and was with the wild beasts; and the angels ministered unto him.

14 Now after that John was put in prison, Jesus came into Galilee, preaching the gospel of the kingdom of God,

15 And saying, The time is fulfilled, and the kingdom of God is at hand: repent ye, and believe the gospel.

16 Now as he walked by the sea of Galilee, he saw Simon and Andrew his brother casting a net into the sea: for they were fishers.

17 And Jesus said unto them, Come ye after me, and I will make you to become fishers of men.

18 And straightway they forsook their nets, and followed him.

19 And when he had gone a little farther thence, he saw James the son of Zebedee, and John his brother, who also were in the ship mending their nets.

20 And straightway he called them: and they left their

1.2 The "messenger" sent into the world before the coming of the Son of God was John the Baptist (v.4).

1.4 "Remission of sins" means the putting away of sins. Not sins covered up, but sins pardoned, never to be brought up again.

1.5 "Confession" - Sins can never be forgiven until there is deep contrition of heart and an acknowledgement of our guilt before God.

1.6 "girdle of a skin about his loins" means a "leather belt around his waist"

1.7 "latchet' means "lace, straps"

1.8 "Holy Ghost" means "Holy Spirit". There is one God with three persons in the Godhead. God the Father (v.11), God the Son (v.1) and God the Holy Spirit (v.8).

1.15 "Repent" -to repent means that we are not only sorry for our sins, but are prepared to turn entirely from them to seek God's salvation. True conversion to God cannot take place without this.

1.17 The evidence of salvation is seen in our desire to tell others about Christ, that they too may trust Him as their Saviour.

1.20 These brothers wanted to follow Christ above

everything else. They made it their number one priority.

1.29 "Forthwith when they were come out.." means "as soon as they were come out"

1.30 "Anon" means "immediately".

1.32 "even" means "evening" and "devils" should read "demons".

1.34 During the time that the Son of God was on earth there seemed to be an increased amount of demonic activity, where it was common for people to be demon possessed. The Lord Jesus had the power to release them from the power of the devil. He still has that power today! Sadly spiritism and devil worship are still present.

1.37 The Lord did not want cheap popularity. He knew that ultimately He would be rejected by the world. He was interested in true conversion, where men and women loved Him from a true heart.

1.38 The Lord Jesus wanted everyone to hear the good news of salvation (see 16.15). He came to save us from the power and consequence of our sins.

1.40 "If you are willing you can make me clean". Although the leper had never seen or known anyone else being cleansed

father Zebedee in the ship with the hired servants, and went after him.

21 And they went into Capernaum; and straightway on the sabbath day he entered into the synagogue, and taught.

22 And they were astonished at his doctrine: for he taught them as one that had authority, and not as the scribes.

23 And there was in their synagogue a man with an unclean spirit; and he cried out,

24 Saying, Let us alone; what have we to do with thee, thou Jesus of Nazareth? art thou come to destroy us? I know thee who thou art, the Holy One of God.

25 And Jesus rebuked him, saying, Hold thy peace, and come out of him.

26 And when the unclean spirit had torn him, and cried with a loud voice, he came out of him.

27 And they were all amazed, insomuch that they questioned among themselves, saying, What thing is this? what new doctrine is this? for with authority commandeth he even the unclean spirits, and they do obey him.

28 And immediately his fame spread abroad throughout all the region round about Galilee.

29 And forthwith, when they were come out of the synagogue, they entered into the house of Simon and Andrew, with James and John.

30 But Simon's wife's mother lay sick of a fever, and anon they tell him of her.

31 And he came and took her by the hand, and lifted her up; and immediately the fever left her, and she ministered unto them.

32 And at even, when the sun did set, they brought unto him all that were diseased, and them that were possessed with devils.

33 And all the city was gathered together at the door.

34 And he healed many that were sick of divers diseases, and cast out many devils; and suffered not the devils to speak, because they knew him.

35 And in the morning, rising up a great while before day, he went out, and departed into a solitary place, and there prayed.

36 And Simon and they that were with him followed after him.

37 And when they had found him, they said unto him, All men seek for thee.

38 And he said unto them, Let us go into the next towns, that I may preach there also: for therefore came I forth.

39 And he preached in their synagogues throughout all Galilee, and cast out devils.

40 And there came a leper to him, beseeching him, and kneeling down to him, and saying unto him, If thou wilt, thou canst make me clean.

41 And Jesus, moved with compassion, put forth his hand, and touched him, and saith unto him, I will; be thou clean.

42 And as soon as he had spoken, immediately the leprosy departed from him, and he was cleansed.

43 And he straitly charged him, and forthwith sent him away;

44 And saith unto him, See thou say nothing to any man: but go thy way, shew thyself to the priest, and offer for thy cleansing those things which Moses commanded, for a testimony unto them.

45 But he went out, and began to publish it much, and to blaze abroad the matter, insomuch that Jesus could no more openly enter into the city, but was without in desert

he did not doubt Christ's power.

Mark 2

1 And again he entered into Capernaum after some days; and it was noised that he was in the house.

2 And straightway many were gathered together, insomuch that there was no room to receive them, no, not so much as about the door: and he preached the word unto them.

3 And they come unto him, bringing one sick of the palsy, which was borne of four.

4 And when they could not come nigh unto him for the press, they uncovered the roof where he was: and when they had broken it up, they let down the bed wherein the sick of the palsy lay.

5 When Jesus saw their faith, he said unto the sick of the palsy, Son, thy sins be forgiven thee.

6 But there was certain of the scribes sitting there, and reasoning in their hearts,

7 Why doth this man thus speak blasphemies? who can forgive sins but God only?

8 And immediately when Jesus perceived in his spirit that they so reasoned within themselves, he said unto them, Why reason ye these things in your hearts?

9 Whether is it easier to say to the sick of the palsy, Thy sins be forgiven thee; or to say, Arise, and take up thy bed, and walk?

10 But that ye may know that the Son of man hath power on earth to forgive sins, (he saith to the sick of the palsy,)

11 I say unto thee, Arise, and take up thy bed, and go thy way into thine house.

12 And immediately he arose, took up the bed, and went forth before them all; insomuch that they were all amazed, and glorified God, saying, We never saw it on this fashion.

2.1 "Noised"- "widely known".

2.3 "Palsy" means "paralysis". "Borne" means "carried".

2.4 "The press" means the crowd of people.

2.5 We would have reversed the process by healing the man before forgiving him. But the man had a bigger problem than being paralysed - he was a sinner before a holy God!

2.10 Forgiveness of sins is possible only through the Lord Jesus Christ. The Pharisees were right in verse 7 - no one but God can forgive sins! What they did not realise was that Jesus is God (c.f. John 1.1; 10.33; 20.28).

2.14 "Receipt of custom" - where taxes were paid.

2.16 "Publicans" were tax collectors.

2.17 A "Physician" is a doctor. Some people do not realise or want to admit they need a doctor. Sadly many sinners feel they have 'no need' of Christ and therefore they remain spiritually ill and are in danger of dying without the great physician - Christ.

2.20 The Lord Jesus was referring to the time when He would be crucified and no longer physically present on earth.

2.21 Trying to sew a new patch of cloth on an old threadbare garment results in the hole getting worse. The Lord Jesus was saying that salvation is not a 'patch-up job' on our sins, but a new start. We need to turn from our old life of sin and accept new life in Christ.

2.24 "Sabbath" - the seventh day was a special day, for God rested on the seventh day in Genesis 1. However the Jews had added laws to the Sabbath that were more than the law of God required. (Compare 7.5-13).

2.28 "Son of Man" is the title of the Lord Jesus Christ He most commonly used of Himself. (Compare 8.31,38; 9.12; 10.33; 13.26,34). It is a title of Messianic authority and power.

13 And he went forth again by the sea side; and all the multitude resorted unto him, and he taught them.
14 And as he passed by, he saw Levi the son of Alphaeus sitting at the receipt of custom, and said unto him, Follow me. And he arose and followed him.
15 And it came to pass, that, as Jesus sat at meat in his house, many publicans and sinners sat also together with Jesus and his disciples: for there were many, and they followed him.
16 And when the scribes and Pharisees saw him eat with publicans and sinners, they said unto his disciples, How is it that he eateth and drinketh with publicans and sinners?
17 When Jesus heard it, he saith unto them, They that are whole have no need of the physician, but they that are sick: I came not to call the righteous, but sinners to repentance.
18 And the disciples of John and of the Pharisees used to fast: and they come and say unto him, Why do the disciples of John and of the Pharisees fast, but thy disciples fast not?
19 And Jesus said unto them, Can the children of the bridechamber fast, while the bridegroom is with them? as long as they have the bridegroom with them, they cannot fast.
20 But the days will come, when the bridegroom shall be taken away from them, and then shall they fast in those days.
21 No man also seweth a piece of new cloth on an old garment: else the new piece that filled it up taketh away from the old, and the rent is made worse.
22 And no man putteth new wine into old bottles: else the new wine doth burst the bottles, and the wine is spilled, and the bottles will be marred: but new wine must be put into new bottles.
23 And it came to pass, that he went through the corn fields on the sabbath day; and his disciples began, as they went, to pluck the ears of corn.
24 And the Pharisees said unto him, Behold, why do they on the sabbath day that which is not lawful?
25 And he said unto them, Have ye never read what David did, when he had need, and was an hungred, he, and they that were with him?
26 How he went into the house of God in the days of Abiathar the high priest, and did eat the shewbread, which is not lawful to eat but for the priests, and gave also to them which were with him?
27 And he said unto them, The sabbath was made for man, and not man for the sabbath:
28 Therefore the Son of man is Lord also of the sabbath.

Mark 3

1 And he entered again into the synagogue; and there was a man there which had a withered hand.

2 And they watched him, whether he would heal him on the sabbath day; that they might accuse him.

3 And he saith unto the man which had the withered hand, Stand forth.

4 And he saith unto them, Is it lawful to do good on the sabbath days, or to do evil? to save life, or to kill? But they held their peace.

5 And when he had looked round about on them with anger, being grieved for the hardness of their hearts, he saith unto the man, Stretch forth thine hand. And he stretched it out: and his hand was restored whole as the other.

6 And the Pharisees went forth, and straightway took counsel with the Herodians against him, how they might destroy him.

7 But Jesus withdrew himself with his disciples to the sea: and a great multitude from Galilee followed him, and from Judaea,

8 And from Jerusalem, and from Idumaea, and from beyond Jordan; and they about Tyre and Sidon, a great multitude, when they had heard what great things he did, came unto him.

9 And he spake to his disciples, that a small ship should wait on him because of the multitude, lest they should throng him.

10 For he had healed many; insomuch that they pressed upon him for to touch him, as many as had plagues.

11 And unclean spirits, when they saw him, fell down before him, and cried, saying, Thou art the Son of God.

12 And he straitly charged them that they should not make him known.

13 And he goeth up into a mountain, and calleth unto him whom he would: and they came unto him.

14 And he ordained twelve, that they should be with him, and that he might send them forth to preach,

15 And to have power to heal sicknesses, and to cast out devils:

16 And Simon he surnamed Peter;

17 And James the son of Zebedee, and John the brother of James; and he surnamed them Boanerges, which is, The sons of thunder:

18 And Andrew, and Philip, and Bartholomew, and Matthew, and Thomas, and James the son of Alphaeus, and Thaddaeus, and Simon the Canaanite,

19 And Judas Iscariot, which also betrayed him: and they went into an house.

3.1 "Withered" means "deformed".

3.6 "Herodians" - those who followed Herod (6.14-28). He was the Roman Caesar's puppet king in charge of Jerusalem and was disliked by the nationalistic Jew. The Pharisees were a very devout, religious Jewish community who disliked the Herodians. However, here enemies unite against the Saviour.

3.8 "Idumaea" - Edom. Modern day Jordan. "Tyre and Sidon" – modern day Lebanon.

3.12 The Lord Jesus never took advantage of any situation for His own ends. He was not here to court fame but to save the world. He did not want lying lips speaking well of Him, for true worship can be acceptable only from true disciples. (John 4.24).

3.22 "Beelzebub" the name they gave the devil.

20 And the multitude cometh together again, so that they could not so much as eat bread.

21 And when his friends heard of it, they went out to lay hold on him: for they said, He is beside himself.

22 And the scribes which came down from Jerusalem said, He hath Beelzebub, and by the prince of the devils casteth he out devils.

23 And he called them unto him, and said unto them in parables, How can Satan cast out Satan?

24 And if a kingdom be divided against itself, that kingdom cannot stand.

25 And if a house be divided against itself, that house cannot stand.

26 And if Satan rise up against himself, and be divided, he cannot stand, but hath an end.

27 No man can enter into a strong man's house, and spoil his goods, except he will first bind the strong man; and then he will spoil his house.

28 Verily I say unto you, All sins shall be forgiven unto the sons of men, and blasphemies wherewith soever they shall blaspheme:

29 But he that shall blaspheme against the Holy Ghost hath never forgiveness, but is in danger of eternal damnation.

30 Because they said, He hath an unclean spirit.

31 There came then his brethren and his mother, and, standing without, sent unto him, calling him.

32 And the multitude sat about him, and they said unto him, Behold, thy mother and thy brethren without seek for thee.

33 And he answered them, saying, Who is my mother, or my brethren?

34 And he looked round about on them which sat about him, and said, Behold my mother and my brethren!

35 For whosoever shall do the will of God, the same is my brother, and my sister, and mother.

3.30 The spirit of Christ was the Holy Spirit of God. To attribute satanic uncleanness to Him was to reject God, His work and His words. These people were in danger of having no further opportunity to get salvation, and ultimately to be punished forever.

3.35 Coming to Jesus Christ for salvation means you are born again into a new family. You have a Father in God and you become His child. You also gain brothers and sisters in the Lord (see John 3.7).

Mark 4

1 And he began again to teach by the sea side: and there was gathered unto him a great multitude, so that he entered into a ship, and sat in the sea; and the whole multitude was by the sea on the land.

2 And he taught them many things by parables, and said unto them in his doctrine,

3 Hearken; Behold, there went out a sower to sow:

4 And it came to pass, as he sowed, some fell by the way side, and the fowls of the air came and devoured it up.

5 And some fell on stony ground, where it had not much

4.2 "Parable" - a story which on the surface is easily understood but behind it is a far more profound meaning about God and His dealings with the world etc.

earth; and immediately it sprang up, because it had no depth of earth:

6 But when the sun was up, it was scorched; and because it had no root, it withered away.

7 And some fell among thorns, and the thorns grew up, and choked it, and it yielded no fruit.

8 And other fell on good ground, and did yield fruit that sprang up and increased; and brought forth, some thirty, and some sixty, and some an hundred.

9 And he said unto them, He that hath ears to hear, let him hear.

10 And when he was alone, they that were about him with the twelve asked of him the parable.

11 And he said unto them, Unto you it is given to know the mystery of the kingdom of God: but unto them that are without, all these things are done in parables:

12 That seeing they may see, and not perceive; and hearing they may hear, and not understand; lest at any time they should be converted, and their sins should be forgiven them.

13 And he said unto them, Know ye not this parable? and how then will ye know all parables?

14 The sower soweth the word.

15 And these are they by the way side, where the word is sown; but when they have heard, Satan cometh immediately, and taketh away the word that was sown in their hearts.

16 And these are they likewise which are sown on stony ground; who, when they have heard the word, immediately receive it with gladness;

17 And have no root in themselves, and so endure but for a time: afterward, when affliction or persecution ariseth for the word's sake, immediately they are offended.

18 And these are they which are sown among thorns; such as hear the word,

19 And the cares of this world, and the deceitfulness of riches, and the lusts of other things entering in, choke the word, and it becometh unfruitful.

20 And these are they which are sown on good ground; such as hear the word, and receive it, and bring forth fruit, some thirtyfold, some sixty, and some an hundred.

21 And he said unto them, Is a candle brought to be put under a bushel, or under a bed? and not to be set on a candlestick?

22 For there is nothing hid, which shall not be manifested; neither was any thing kept secret, but that it should come abroad.

23 If any man have ears to hear, let him hear.

24 And he said unto them, Take heed what ye hear: with what measure ye mete, it shall be measured to you: and

4.14 "The word" means the Word of God. God's word is now complete and is composed of sixty-six books that make up the Bible.

4.14-20 The four types of soil speak of the four types of response to the reading and preaching of the Word of God.

Wayside: lazy hearer - does not spend too much time thinking about what he has heard. Soon after he has heard the Word the devil takes away anything that caused him to be concerned.

Stony soil: cowardly hearer - realises the importance of what he has heard but knows that he will receive a lot of opposition if he turns to God for salvation.

Thorny soil: superficial but unrepentant hearer - seems keen to become a Christian, but the world and all it has to offer overrides and overwhelms his thoughts.

Good ground: true hearer - hears, repents, believes and receives eternal life.

4.21 "Bushel" - a vessel for measuring volume.

4.22 The principle here is that we cannot hide anything from God.

4.24 "Measure ye mete" means "what standard you apply".

4.26 This parable is unique to Mark's gospel.

4.28 The process from seed to first green shoot to a full head of corn is a work of God in nature. The work of salvation in relation to the kingdom of heaven is also a work of God. Man has no ground to boast! (Ephesians 2.8).

4.29 A sickle is a tool used to cut down wheat or barley.

4.35 "Let us pass over unto the other side" Now read 5.1! When the Lord said He was going to the other side He meant it. Christ is present with those who trust in Him through every storm of life.

5.1 Gadarenes- a region in the south east side of Lake Galilee

5.2 "Unclean spirit" - contrast with 3.30.

unto you that hear shall more be given.

25 For he that hath, to him shall be given: and he that hath not, from him shall be taken even that which he hath.

26 And he said, So is the kingdom of God, as if a man should cast seed into the ground;

27 And should sleep, and rise night and day, and the seed should spring and grow up, he knoweth not how.

28 For the earth bringeth forth fruit of herself; first the blade, then the ear, after that the full corn in the ear.

29 But when the fruit is brought forth, immediately he putteth in the sickle, because the harvest is come.

30 And he said, Whereunto shall we liken the kingdom of God? or with what comparison shall we compare it?

31 It is like a grain of mustard seed, which, when it is sown in the earth, is less than all the seeds that be in the earth:

32 But when it is sown, it groweth up, and becometh greater than all herbs, and shooteth out great branches; so that the fowls of the air may lodge under the shadow of it.

33 And with many such parables spake he the word unto them, as they were able to hear it.

34 But without a parable spake he not unto them: and when they were alone, he expounded all things to his disciples.

35 And the same day, when the even was come, he saith unto them, Let us pass over unto the other side.

36 And when they had sent away the multitude, they took him even as he was in the ship. And there were also with him other little ships.

37 And there arose a great storm of wind, and the waves beat into the ship, so that it was now full.

38 And he was in the hinder part of the ship, asleep on a pillow: and they awake him, and say unto him, Master, carest thou not that we perish?

39 And he arose, and rebuked the wind, and said unto the sea, Peace, be still. And the wind ceased, and there was a great calm.

40 And he said unto them, Why are ye so fearful? how is it that ye have no faith?

41 And they feared exceedingly, and said one to another, What manner of man is this, that even the wind and the sea obey him?

Mark 5

1 And they came over unto the other side of the sea, into the country of the Gadarenes.

2 And when he was come out of the ship, immediately there met him out of the tombs a man with an unclean

spirit,

3 Who had his dwelling among the tombs; and no man could bind him, no, not with chains:

4 Because that he had been often bound with fetters and chains, and the chains had been plucked asunder by him, and the fetters broken in pieces: neither could any man tame him.

5 And always, night and day, he was in the mountains, and in the tombs, crying, and cutting himself with stones.

6 But when he saw Jesus afar off, he ran and worshipped him,

7 And cried with a loud voice, and said, What have I to do with thee, Jesus, thou Son of the most high God? I adjure thee by God, that thou torment me not.

8 For he said unto him, Come out of the man, thou unclean spirit.

9 And he asked him, What is thy name? And he answered, saying, My name is Legion: for we are many.

10 And he besought him much that he would not send them away out of the country.

11 Now there was there nigh unto the mountains a great herd of swine feeding.

12 And all the devils besought him, saying, Send us into the swine, that we may enter into them.

13 And forthwith Jesus gave them leave. And the unclean spirits went out, and entered into the swine: and the herd ran violently down a steep place into the sea, (they were about two thousand;) and were choked in the sea.

14 And they that fed the swine fled, and told it in the city, and in the country. And they went out to see what it was that was done.

15 And they come to Jesus, and see him that was possessed with the devil, and had the legion, sitting, and clothed, and in his right mind: and they were afraid.

16 And they that saw it told them how it befell to him that was possessed with the devil, and also concerning the swine.

17 And they began to pray him to depart out of their coasts.

18 And when he was come into the ship, he that had been possessed with the devil prayed him that he might be with him.

19 Howbeit Jesus suffered him not, but saith unto him, Go home to thy friends, and tell them how great things the Lord hath done for thee, and hath had compassion on thee.

20 And he departed, and began to publish in Decapolis how great things Jesus had done for him: and all men did marvel.

21 And when Jesus was passed over again by ship unto

5.7 "adjure" means "put on oath"

5.9 'Legion' - A legion was a unit in the Roman army of between three and six thousand men. This man had given himself over to many demons. This explains his name and desperate lifestyle.

5.15 There are no cases too hard for God. All can be saved and put in their "right mind".

5.17 To these men, the welfare of their pigs was more important than the miracle wrought on the once demon possessed man.

5.20 "Publish" - speaking about Christ is a mark of a real Christian.

5.25 This lady had been hemorrhaging for twelve years.

5.26 Just as this woman could find no help in men, so we too need to turn away from men to Christ for help.

5.29 "Straightway" - The woman did not need to wait to receive help. Similarly, salvation is immediately given to the seeking sinner when it is asked for in true repentance.

5.30 "Virtue" means "power"

5.32 He knew who had touched Him but the question was to elicit her deepest desire and expression of faith.

5.34 "Go in (into) peace and be whole" - The woman received peace with God and was cured of her illness. She received far more than restored health - she received salvation!

the other side, much people gathered unto him: and he was nigh unto the sea.

22 And, behold, there cometh one of the rulers of the synagogue, Jairus by name; and when he saw him, he fell at his feet,

23 And besought him greatly, saying, My little daughter lieth at the point of death: I pray thee, come and lay thy hands on her, that she may be healed; and she shall live.

24 And Jesus went with him; and much people followed him, and thronged him.

25 And a certain woman, which had an issue of blood twelve years,

26 And had suffered many things of many physicians, and had spent all that she had, and was nothing bettered, but rather grew worse,

27 When she had heard of Jesus, came in the press behind, and touched his garment.

28 For she said, If I may touch but his clothes, I shall be whole.

29 And straightway the fountain of her blood was dried up; and she felt in her body that she was healed of that plague.

30 And Jesus, immediately knowing in himself that virtue had gone out of him, turned him about in the press, and said, Who touched my clothes?

31 And his disciples said unto him, Thou seest the multitude thronging thee, and sayest thou, Who touched me?

32 And he looked round about to see her that had done this thing.

33 But the woman fearing and trembling, knowing what was done in her, came and fell down before him, and told him all the truth.

34 And he said unto her, Daughter, thy faith hath made thee whole; go in peace, and be whole of thy plague.

35 While he yet spake, there came from the ruler of the synagogue's house certain which said, Thy daughter is dead: why troublest thou the Master any further?

36 As soon as Jesus heard the word that was spoken, he saith unto the ruler of the synagogue, Be not afraid, only believe.

37 And he suffered no man to follow him, save Peter, and James, and John the brother of James.

38 And he cometh to the house of the ruler of the synagogue, and seeth the tumult, and them that wept and wailed greatly.

39 And when he was come in, he saith unto them, Why make ye this ado, and weep? the damsel is not dead, but sleepeth.

40 And they laughed him to scorn. But when he had put

them all out, he taketh the father and the mother of the damsel, and them that were with him, and entereth in where the damsel was lying.

41 And he took the damsel by the hand, and said unto her, Talitha cumi; which is, being interpreted, Damsel, I say unto thee, arise.

42 And straightway the damsel arose, and walked; for she was of the age of twelve years. And they were astonished with a great astonishment.

43 And he charged them straitly that no man should know it; and commanded that something should be given her to eat.

5.42 The Bible records three times in detail the Lord raising the dead, (see also Luke 7.14; John 11.43) although He also did this on other occasions Luke 7.22).

Mark 6

1 And he went out from thence, and came into his own country; and his disciples follow him.

2 And when the sabbath day was come, he began to teach in the synagogue: and many hearing him were astonished, saying, From whence hath this man these things? and what wisdom is this which is given unto him, that even such mighty works are wrought by his hands?

3 Is not this the carpenter, the son of Mary, the brother of James, and Joses, and of Juda, and Simon? and are not his sisters here with us? And they were offended at him.

4 But Jesus, said unto them, A prophet is not without honour, but in his own country, and among his own kin, and in his own house.

5 And he could there do no mighty work, save that he laid his hands upon a few sick folk, and healed them.

6 And he marvelled because of their unbelief. And he went round about the villages, teaching.

7 And he called unto him the twelve, and began to send them forth by two and two; and gave them power over unclean spirits;

8 And commanded them that they should take nothing for their journey, save a staff only; no scrip, no bread, no money in their purse:

9 But be shod with sandals; and not put on two coats.

10 And he said unto them, In what place soever ye enter into an house, there abide till ye depart from that place.

11 And whosoever shall not receive you, nor hear you, when ye depart thence, shake off the dust under your feet for a testimony against them. Verily I say unto you, It shall be more tolerable for Sodom and Gomorrha in the day of judgment, than for that city.

12 And they went out, and preached that men should repent.

13 And they cast out many devils, and anointed with oil

6.4 "Kin" means "family"

6.5 The Lord Jesus never did anything contrary to mans' free will. If they did not want blessing and salvation He would not force it upon them. However, to reject God's offer of salvation means that we will ultimately face the punishment for our sins in the lake of fire (Revelation 20.15).

6.8 "Staff" - a large walking stick. "Scrip" - a small bag.

6.11 The fate of Sodom and Gomorrah is recorded in the book of Genesis chapter 19. They are presented in the Bible as evil cities, which were judged by God.

6.12 The message of the disciples never changed! See 1.4,15.

many that were sick, and healed them.

14 And king Herod heard of him; (for his name was spread abroad:) and he said, That John the Baptist was risen from the dead, and therefore mighty works do shew forth themselves in him.

15 Others said, That it is Elias. And others said, That it is a prophet, or as one of the prophets.

6.16 An example of a man with a troubled conscience!

16 But when Herod heard thereof, he said, It is John, whom I beheaded: he is risen from the dead.

17 For Herod himself had sent forth and laid hold upon John, and bound him in prison for Herodias' sake, his brother Philip's wife: for he had married her.

18 For John had said unto Herod, It is not lawful for thee to have thy brother's wife.

19 Therefore Herodias had a quarrel against him, and would have killed him; but she could not:

6.20 Herod regarded John as a good, godly wise man. However he did not like the truth (see v.18).

20 For Herod feared John, knowing that he was a just man and an holy, and observed him; and when he heard him, he did many things, and heard him gladly.

21 And when a convenient day was come, that Herod on his birthday made a supper to his lords, high captains, and chief estates of Galilee;

22 And when the daughter of the said Herodias came in, and danced, and pleased Herod and them that sat with him, the king said unto the damsel, Ask of me whatsoever thou wilt, and I will give it thee.

23 And he sware unto her, Whatsoever thou shalt ask of me, I will give it thee, unto the half of my kingdom.

6.24 Exposure of her gross sin (v18) by John brought out real anger and wicked intentions.

24 And she went forth, and said unto her mother, What shall I ask? And she said, The head of John the Baptist.

25 And she came in straightway with haste unto the king, and asked, saying, I will that thou give me by and by in a charger the head of John the Baptist.

6.25 "Charger" means "a large plate".

6.26 The king's pride was more important to him than justice.

26 And the king was exceeding sorry; yet for his oath's sake, and for their sakes which sat with him, he would not reject her.

27 And immediately the king sent an executioner, and commanded his head to be brought: and he went and beheaded him in the prison,

6.28 This story illustrates the world's opposition to those who present the truth of God 's Word.

28 And brought his head in a charger, and gave it to the damsel: and the damsel gave it to her mother.

29 And when his disciples heard of it, they came and took up his corpse, and laid it in a tomb.

30 And the apostles gathered themselves together unto Jesus, and told him all things, both what they had done, and what they had taught.

6.30 Similarly, sometimes we as Christians can find ourselves in circumstances we cannot understand or change but we can "tell Jesus" about it.

31 And he said unto them, Come ye yourselves apart into a desert place, and rest a while: for there were many coming and going, and they had no leisure so much as to eat.

32 And they departed into a desert place by ship

privately.

33 And the people saw them departing, and many knew him, and ran afoot thither out of all cities, and outwent them, and came together unto him.

34 And Jesus, when he came out, saw much people, and was moved with compassion toward them, because they were as sheep not having a shepherd: and he began to teach them many things.

35 And when the day was now far spent, his disciples came unto him, and said, This is a desert place, and now the time is far passed:

36 Send them away, that they may go into the country round about, and into the villages, and buy themselves bread: for they have nothing to eat.

37 He answered and said unto them, Give ye them to eat. And they say unto him, Shall we go and buy two hundred pennyworth of bread, and give them to eat?

38 He saith unto them, How many loaves have ye? go and see. And when they knew, they say, Five, and two fishes.

39 And he commanded them to make all sit down by companies upon the green grass.

40 And they sat down in ranks, by hundreds, and by fifties.

41 And when he had taken the five loaves and the two fishes, he looked up to heaven, and blessed, and brake the loaves, and gave them to his disciples to set before them; and the two fishes divided he among them all.

42 And they did all eat, and were filled.

43 And they took up twelve baskets full of the fragments, and of the fishes.

44 And they that did eat of the loaves were about five thousand men.

45 And straightway he constrained his disciples to get into the ship, and to go to the other side before unto Bethsaida, while he sent away the people.

46 And when he had sent them away, he departed into a mountain to pray.

47 And when even was come, the ship was in the midst of the sea, and he alone on the land.

48 And he saw them toiling in rowing; for the wind was contrary unto them: and about the fourth watch of the night he cometh unto them, walking upon the sea, and would have passed by them.

49 But when they saw him walking upon the sea, they supposed it had been a spirit, and cried out:

50 For they all saw him, and were troubled. And immediately he talked with them, and saith unto them, Be of good cheer: it is I; be not afraid.

51 And he went up unto them into the ship; and the wind ceased: and they were sore amazed in themselves beyond

6.34 The Lord Jesus was no hard-hearted leader. His compassion for their material needs is seen in 8.2. But here it was their spiritual need that concerned Him most. He longed that they all might be able to say, 'The Lord Jesus is my shepherd'.

6.37 One penny was a day's wage for a working man (Matthew 20.2).

6.42 As the disciples kept coming to the Lord Jesus for provision the loaves and fishes never ran out. In His hands the food multiplied. There is no limit to His power. He can meet our every need.

6.43 There was plenty left over. The physical bread speaks of the spiritual food that God can give to the spiritually starved soul. The Lord Jesus said, "I am the bread of life". There is no limit to the provision of Christ. He can satisfy the void in our lives.

6.48 "He saw them". It was dark, and John's Gospel tells us they were two miles out! This proves that the Lord Jesus, as God, sees everything. Whatever our circumstances are He knows all about them and wants us to allow Him to enter into them.

6.51 "Sore amazed" means "greatly astonished".

measure, and wondered.

52 For they considered not the miracle of the loaves: for their heart was hardened.

53 And when they had passed over, they came into the land of Gennesaret, and drew to the shore.

54 And when they were come out of the ship, straightway they knew him,

55 And ran through that whole region round about, and began to carry about in beds those that were sick, where they heard he was.

56 And whithersoever he entered, into villages, or cities, or country, they laid the sick in the streets, and besought him that they might touch if it were but the border of his garment: and as many as touched him were made whole.

Mark 7

1 Then came together unto him the Pharisees, and certain of the scribes, which came from Jerusalem.

2 And when they saw some of his disciples eat bread with defiled, that is to say, with unwashen, hands, they found fault.

3 For the Pharisees, and all the Jews, except they wash their hands oft, eat not, holding the tradition of the elders.

4 And when they come from the market, except they wash, they eat not. And many other things there be, which they have received to hold, as the washing of cups, and pots, brasen vessels, and of tables.

5 Then the Pharisees and scribes asked him, Why walk not thy disciples according to the tradition of the elders, but eat bread with unwashen hands?

6 He answered and said unto them, Well hath Esaias prophesied of you hypocrites, as it is written, This people honoureth me with their lips, but their heart is far from me.

7 Howbeit in vain do they worship me, teaching for doctrines the commandments of men.

8 For laying aside the commandment of God, ye hold the tradition of men, as the washing of pots and cups: and many other such like things ye do.

9 And he said unto them, Full well ye reject the commandment of God, that ye may keep your own tradition.

10 For Moses said, Honour thy father and thy mother; and, Whoso curseth father or mother, let him die the death:

11 But ye say, If a man shall say to his father or mother, It is Corban, that is to say, a gift, by whatsoever thou mightest be profited by me; he shall be free.

7.4 Basic cleanliness is important, but here the Pharisees took it a step further by making it have religious significance. The so-called religions often "find fault" (v.2) with external things. They value ritual over a relationship with Christ.

7.5 The "tradition of the elders" had become more important than the Word of God. The disciples were not doing anything contrary to the command of the Old Testament Scripture.

7.8-9 There were two faults exposed by the Lord. The Pharisees and Scribes had, firstly, laid to one side the Word of God, and, secondly, replaced it with tradition. We should beware of religions that are merely based on human ideas and traditions and not solely on the Bible.

7.11 "Corban" was an offering to God of any kind, particularly in the fulfillment of a vow. Traditions around this allowed objects and even people to be considered "Corban" or hallowed to God by a vow. This allowed some to exempt themselves from any inconvenient obligation, such as obeying parents, under plea of Corban. It was that rule and tradition that the Lord reprehended.

12 And ye suffer him no more to do ought for his father or his mother;

13 Making the word of God of none effect through your tradition, which ye have delivered: and many such like things do ye.

14 And when he had called all the people unto him, he said unto them, Hearken unto me every one of you, and understand:

15 There is nothing from without a man, that entering into him can defile him: but the things which come out of him, those are they that defile the man.

16 If any man have ears to hear, let him hear.

17 And when he was entered into the house from the people, his disciples asked him concerning the parable.

18 And he saith unto them, Are ye so without understanding also? Do ye not perceive, that whatsoever thing from without entereth into the man, it cannot defile him;

19 Because it entereth not into his heart, but into the belly, and goeth out into the draught, purging all meats?

20 And he said, That which cometh out of the man, that defileth the man.

21 For from within, out of the heart of men, proceed evil thoughts, adulteries, fornications, murders,

22 Thefts, covetousness, wickedness, deceit, lasciviousness, an evil eye, blasphemy, pride, foolishness:

23 All these evil things come from within, and defile the man.

24 And from thence he arose, and went into the borders of Tyre and Sidon, and entered into an house, and would have no man know it: but he could not be hid.

25 For a certain woman, whose young daughter had an unclean spirit, heard of him, and came and fell at his feet:

26 The woman was a Greek, a Syrophenician by nation; and she besought him that he would cast forth the devil out of her daughter.

27 But Jesus said unto her, Let the children first be filled: for it is not meet to take the children's bread, and to cast it unto the dogs.

28 And she answered and said unto him, Yes, Lord: yet the dogs under the table eat of the children's crumbs.

29 And he said unto her, For this saying go thy way; the devil is gone out of thy daughter.

30 And when she was come to her house, she found the devil gone out, and her daughter laid upon the bed.

31 And again, departing from the coasts of Tyre and Sidon, he came unto the sea of Galilee, through the midst of the coasts of Decapolis.

32 And they bring unto him one that was deaf, and had

7.15 The Lord Jesus rejected the theory that we are merely the product of our 'environment'. The problem, He said, lay not outside ourselves, but within, as we all have a sinful nature – see Romans 3.23.

7.19 "Draught" means "latrine" (lavatory). "Purging all meats" - the food is clean. The problem addressed here is that of the sinful heart (see v.21).

7.21 "Fornication" means the sexual act before marriage. Adultery is infidelity whilst married.

7.22 "Lasciviousness" means "sensuality". "An evil eye" means "envy with a view to another's downfall".

7.26 Syrophenician - a Syrian from Phonecia. Phonecia was a narrow strip of land between the Mediterranean Sea and the Lebanon mountains.

7.28 This section has often been misunderstood. The Lord was never racist or rude. Rather He was leading this woman to acknowledge her true position as an undeserving outside case desperate for blessing. Christ always blessed those who came in their need, and were prepared to acknowledge Him as Lord. This woman's daughter was immediately healed.

7.33 "Aside from the multitude" - the man's healing was personal and individual. The Lord Jesus took him away from the influence of the crowd. Salvation is a personal and individual issue. He allowed the Lord to put His finger on the problem - his ears and tongue. The Lord can put His finger on the problem in your life and mine.

7.36 The Lord Jesus was not only powerful, He was also humble. Mark records occasions Jesus asked, (often after He had performed a miracle that no other man had ever done or ever could do), that it should not be publicised. He sought no worldly fame. (See 1.34,44; 3.12; 5.43; 8.26,30; 9.30).

7.37 Exclamations of astonishment at Christ were common (see 1.27; 2.12; 4.41).

8.3 "Divers of them" can read "some of them".

8.9 Christ never sent anyone away empty.

an impediment in his speech; and they beseech him to put his hand upon him.

33 And he took him aside from the multitude, and put his fingers into his ears, and he spit, and touched his tongue;

34 And looking up to heaven, he sighed, and saith unto him, Ephphatha, that is, Be opened.

35 And straightway his ears were opened, and the string of his tongue was loosed, and he spake plain.

36 And he charged them that they should tell no man: but the more he charged them, so much the more a great deal they published it;

37 And were beyond measure astonished, saying, He hath done all things well: he maketh both the deaf to hear, and the dumb to speak.

Mark 8

1 In those days the multitude being very great, and having nothing to eat, Jesus called his disciples unto him, and saith unto them,

2 I have compassion on the multitude, because they have now been with me three days, and have nothing to eat:

3 And if I send them away fasting to their own houses, they will faint by the way: for divers of them came from far.

4 And his disciples answered him, From whence can a man satisfy these men with bread here in the wilderness?

5 And he asked them, How many loaves have ye? And they said, Seven.

6 And he commanded the people to sit down on the ground: and he took the seven loaves, and gave thanks, and brake, and gave to his disciples to set before them; and they did set them before the people.

7 And they had a few small fishes: and he blessed, and commanded to set them also before them.

8 So they did eat, and were filled: and they took up of the broken meat that was left seven baskets.

9 And they that had eaten were about four thousand: and he sent them away.

10 And straightway he entered into a ship with his disciples, and came into the parts of Dalmanutha.

11 And the Pharisees came forth, and began to question with him, seeking of him a sign from heaven, tempting him.

12 And he sighed deeply in his spirit, and saith, Why doth this generation seek after a sign? verily I say unto you, There shall no sign be given unto this generation.

13 And he left them, and entering into the ship again departed to the other side.

14 Now the disciples had forgotten to take bread, neither had they in the ship with them more than one loaf.

15 And he charged them, saying, Take heed, beware of the leaven of the Pharisees, and of the leaven of Herod.

16 And they reasoned among themselves, saying, It is because we have no bread.

17 And when Jesus knew it, he saith unto them, Why reason ye, because ye have no bread? perceive ye not yet, neither understand? have ye your heart yet hardened?

18 Having eyes, see ye not? and having ears, hear ye not? and do ye not remember?

19 When I brake the five loaves among five thousand, how many baskets full of fragments took ye up? They say unto him, Twelve.

20 And when the seven among four thousand, how many baskets full of fragments took ye up? And they said, Seven.

21 And he said unto them, How is it that ye do not understand?

22 And he cometh to Bethsaida; and they bring a blind man unto him, and besought him to touch him.

23 And he took the blind man by the hand, and led him out of the town; and when he had spit on his eyes, and put his hands upon him, he asked him if he saw ought.

24 And he looked up, and said, I see men as trees, walking.

25 After that he put his hands again upon his eyes, and made him look up: and he was restored, and saw every man clearly.

26 And he sent him away to his house, saying, Neither go into the town, nor tell it to any in the town.

27 And Jesus went out, and his disciples, into the towns of Caesarea Philippi: and by the way he asked his disciples, saying unto them, Whom do men say that I am?

28 And they answered, John the Baptist; but some say, Elias; and others, One of the prophets.

29 And he saith unto them, But whom say ye that I am? And Peter answereth and saith unto him, Thou art the Christ.

30 And he charged them that they should tell no man of him.

31 And he began to teach them, that the Son of man must suffer many things, and be rejected of the elders, and of the chief priests, and scribes, and be killed, and after three days rise again.

32 And he spake that saying openly. And Peter took him, and began to rebuke him.

33 But when he had turned about and looked on his disciples, he rebuked Peter, saying, Get thee behind me, Satan: for thou savourest not the things that be of God,

8.15 "Leaven" means yeast. It is used in the Bible as an illustration of evil. Just as yeast puffs up a loaf, so the Pharisees were guilty of pride and hypocrisy: the Herodians of profligate living (6.17).

8.18 Like the disciples we so quickly forget His power, and, taken up with the physical and the natural, don't hear and see the lessons God would teach us concerning the spiritual and the eternal.

8.25 The Lord could have healed him with or without one touch! The lesson to us is the need to "look up" for salvation.

8.29 "Christ" is the Greek word for the Hebrew word 'Messiah'. It means the 'Anointed'. To some men He was only a prophet, but to the disciples He was the King of kings.

8.31 See 9.9,12,31; 10.33-34; 12.6-8; 14.8,18,27-28,42. The Lord knew that He would be rejected by men and crucified, but also knew that He would rise again from the dead.

8.33 "Savourest" means "are concerned about". Strong words were used here to Peter. But it was Satan who wanted to stop the Lord Jesus from reaching the Cross. The eternal plan of God demanded that His Son should die for the world. Sin could only be forgiven if

Christ took the punishment for all sin.

8.34 Self-denial is the first step of discipleship. Not monastic living, but allowing the Lord Jesus to be in control of our life.

8.37 The Lord Jesus is teaching that our most valuable possession is our soul, and nothing the world has to offer can be compared with it.

8.38 This is the first mention in Mark of the Lord Jesus returning to earth, not now as Saviour, but as Judge.

9.1 The "some" referred to here were Peter, James and John (vv.2-9). They were going to see a preview of His future glory when He would come to set up His kingdom.

9.3 "Fuller" - a tradesman who cleaned cloth for a living.

9.4 Elias is the Greek name for Elijah the Prophet (I Kings 17 – 2 Kings 2).

9.5 Peter gave the Lord Jesus place, but made a mistake in including Moses and Elias in his proposition. The voice of God was heard from Heaven (v.7) to set the record straight. No one can be compared to His Son! He stands unique among men.

but the things that be of men.

34 And when he had called the people unto him with his disciples also, he said unto them, Whosoever will come after me, let him deny himself, and take up his cross, and follow me.

35 For whosoever will save his life shall lose it; but whosoever shall lose his life for my sake and the gospel's, the same shall save it.

36 For what shall it profit a man, if he shall gain the whole world, and lose his own soul?

37 Or what shall a man give in exchange for his soul?

38 Whosoever therefore shall be ashamed of me and of my words in this adulterous and sinful generation; of him also shall the Son of man be ashamed, when he cometh in the glory of his Father with the holy angels.

Mark 9

1 And he said unto them, Verily I say unto you, That there be some of them that stand here, which shall not taste of death, till they have seen the kingdom of God come with power.

2 And after six days Jesus taketh with him Peter, and James, and John, and leadeth them up into an high mountain apart by themselves: and he was transfigured before them.

3 And his raiment became shining, exceeding white as snow; so as no fuller on earth can white them.

4 And there appeared unto them Elias with Moses: and they were talking with Jesus.

5 And Peter answered and said to Jesus, Master, it is good for us to be here: and let us make three tabernacles; one for thee, and one for Moses, and one for Elias.

6 For he wist not what to say; for they were sore afraid.

7 And there was a cloud that overshadowed them: and a voice came out of the cloud, saying, This is my beloved Son: hear him.

8 And suddenly, when they had looked round about, they saw no man any more, save Jesus only with themselves.

9 And as they came down from the mountain, he charged them that they should tell no man what things they had seen, till the Son of man were risen from the dead.

10 And they kept that saying with themselves, questioning one with another what the rising from the dead should mean.

11 And they asked him, saying, Why say the scribes that Elias must first come?

12 And he answered and told them, Elias verily cometh first, and restoreth all things; and how it is written of the Son of man, that he must suffer many things, and be set at nought.

13 But I say unto you, That Elias is indeed come, and they have done unto him whatsoever they listed, as it is written of him.

14 And when he came to his disciples, he saw a great multitude about them, and the scribes questioning with them.

15 And straightway all the people, when they beheld him, were greatly amazed, and running to him saluted him.

16 And he asked the scribes, What question ye with them?

17 And one of the multitude answered and said, Master, I have brought unto thee my son, which hath a dumb spirit;

18 And wheresoever he taketh him, he teareth him: and he foameth, and gnasheth with his teeth, and pineth away: and I spake to thy disciples that they should cast him out; and they could not.

19 He answereth him, and saith, O faithless generation, how long shall I be with you? how long shall I suffer you? bring him unto me.

20 And they brought him unto him: and when he saw him, straightway the spirit tare him; and he fell on the ground, and wallowed foaming.

21 And he asked his father, How long is it ago since this came unto him? And he said, Of a child.

22 And ofttimes it hath cast him into the fire, and into the waters, to destroy him: but if thou canst do any thing, have compassion on us, and help us.

23 Jesus said unto him, If thou canst believe, all things are possible to him that believeth.

24 And straightway the father of the child cried out, and said with tears, Lord, I believe; help thou mine unbelief.

25 When Jesus saw that the people came running together, he rebuked the foul spirit, saying unto him, Thou dumb and deaf spirit, I charge thee, come out of him, and enter no more into him.

26 And the spirit cried, and rent him sore, and came out of him: and he was as one dead; insomuch that many said, He is dead.

27 But Jesus took him by the hand, and lifted him up; and he arose.

28 And when he was come into the house, his disciples asked him privately, Why could not we cast him out?

29 And he said unto them, This kind can come forth by nothing, but by prayer and fasting.

30 And they departed thence, and passed through Galilee;

9.13 The Lord Jesus is discussing John the Baptist in these verses. He was born in a similar period to Elijah and had a very similar task. (Matthew 17.10-13; Luke 1.17).
"listed' means "willed, pleased or liked"

9.22 The man here doubted the compassion and power of Christ ("if thou canst do anything"). Compassion was one thing the man did not need to ask of the Lord (1.41; 5.19; 6.34; 8.2).

9.23 The Lord showed the problem lay not with His lack of power but with the man's lack of faith. He said, "If you can believe".

9.25 Any other man would have waited until the maximum audience had arrived before performing the miracle. The Lord Jesus had not come to receive applause but to provide and offer salvation for the world.

9.32 The Lord Jesus foretold His resurrection on many occasions, but the disciples still did not understand that if there was to be any salvation the Lord Jesus had to die for the world. This truth still escaped them (see v.10).

9.35 The Lord Jesus was teaching that true greatness is seen in true humility. His greatness was declared by His willingness, as Son of God, to minister to men and even stoop to Calvary where He would die for the sin of the world.

9.43 The Lord Jesus was not teaching self mutilation. He was warning against allowing our hands (what we do), our feet (where we go) and our eyes (what we look at and therefore think about) to be vehicles for sin. He used strong language to indicate how seriously we should treat this matter. It will have eternal consequences!

and he would not that any man should know it.

31 For he taught his disciples, and said unto them, The Son of man is delivered into the hands of men, and they shall kill him; and after that he is killed, he shall rise the third day.

32 But they understood not that saying, and were afraid to ask him.

33 And he came to Capernaum: and being in the house he asked them, What was it that ye disputed among yourselves by the way?

34 But they held their peace: for by the way they had disputed among themselves, who should be the greatest.

35 And he sat down, and called the twelve, and saith unto them, If any man desire to be first, the same shall be last of all, and servant of all.

36 And he took a child, and set him in the midst of them: and when he had taken him in his arms, he said unto them,

37 Whosoever shall receive one of such children in my name, receiveth me: and whosoever shall receive me, receiveth not me, but him that sent me.

38 And John answered him, saying, Master, we saw one casting out devils in thy name, and he followeth not us: and we forbad him, because he followeth not us.

39 But Jesus said, Forbid him not: for there is no man which shall do a miracle in my name, that can lightly speak evil of me.

40 For he that is not against us is on our part.

41 For whosoever shall give you a cup of water to drink in my name, because ye belong to Christ, verily I say unto you, he shall not lose his reward.

42 And whosoever shall offend one of these little ones that believe in me, it is better for him that a millstone were hanged about his neck, and he were cast into the sea.

43 And if thy hand offend thee, cut it off: it is better for thee to enter into life maimed, than having two hands to go into hell, into the fire that never shall be quenched:

44 Where their worm dieth not, and the fire is not quenched.

45 And if thy foot offend thee, cut it off: it is better for thee to enter halt into life, than having two feet to be cast into hell, into the fire that never shall be quenched:

46 Where their worm dieth not, and the fire is not quenched.

47 And if thine eye offend thee, pluck it out: it is better for thee to enter into the kingdom of God with one eye, than having two eyes to be cast into hell fire:

48 Where their worm dieth not, and the fire is not quenched.

49 For every one shall be salted with fire, and every sacrifice shall be salted with salt.
50 Salt is good: but if the salt have lost his saltness, wherewith will ye season it? Have salt in yourselves, and have peace one with another.

Mark 10

1 And he arose from thence, and cometh into the coasts of Judaea by the farther side of Jordan: and the people resort unto him again; and, as he was wont, he taught them again.
2 And the Pharisees came to him, and asked him, Is it lawful for a man to put away his wife? tempting him.
3 And he answered and said unto them, What did Moses command you?
4 And they said, Moses suffered to write a bill of divorcement, and to put her away.
5 And Jesus answered and said unto them, For the hardness of your heart he wrote you this precept.
6 But from the beginning of the creation God made them male and female.
7 For this cause shall a man leave his father and mother, and cleave to his wife;
8 And they twain shall be one flesh: so then they are no more twain, but one flesh.
9 What therefore God hath joined together, let not man put asunder.
10 And in the house his disciples asked him again of the same matter.
11 And he saith unto them, Whosoever shall put away his wife, and marry another, committeth adultery against her.
12 And if a woman shall put away her husband, and be married to another, she committeth adultery.
13 And they brought young children to him, that he should touch them: and his disciples rebuked those that brought them.
14 But when Jesus saw it, he was much displeased, and said unto them, Suffer the little children to come unto me, and forbid them not: for of such is the kingdom of God.
15 Verily I say unto you, Whosoever shall not receive the kingdom of God as a little child, he shall not enter therein.
16 And he took them up in his arms, put his hands upon them, and blessed them.
17 And when he was gone forth into the way, there came one running, and kneeled to him, and asked him, Good Master, what shall I do that I may inherit eternal life?

9.50 Salt has a distinctive taste and is also a preservative. The Lord Jesus was stating that Christians should be distinctive by their holy life and character and be a moral 'preservative' in society.

10.11-12 The Lord Jesus was saying that remarriage after divorce is adultery. God alone can dissolve the marriage bond through death (c.f. 6.18).

10.13 The disciples and the people in verse 48 thought they knew best who should come to Christ. The Lord Jesus came for all men and women and all boys and girls. None are excluded.

10.15 God's salvation is to be received in child-like faith and trust.

10.18 Here the Lord Jesus was not denying His deity but He was exposing the loose way the man uses the term "good". The ruler obviously considered himself good (see Matthew 19.16; Romans 3.12).

10.20-22 The Lord Jesus loved him despite the fact the man could not see the problem of his sin. Sadly he left without receiving salvation from Christ.

10.24 If wealth kept this man from salvation, we need to ask ourselves what might we be putting before the salvation of our soul? Notice it was not riches and wealth that was the problem but that he "trusted in riches".

10.25 An example of hyperbole designed to astonish His audience. Salvation is not a human possibility, just as a camel going through a needle is not a possibility. We cannot save ourselves!

10.26 "Saved" is an important Bible word (Acts 4.12; 16.30; Romans 10.9). It carries the idea that we are in danger and need to be rescued from our sins, an empty purposeless life, and eternal punishment.

10.34 The Lord gave graphic detail of His sufferings. This had been foretold many

18 And Jesus said unto him, Why callest thou me good? there is none good but one, that is, God.
19 Thou knowest the commandments, Do not commit adultery, Do not kill, Do not steal, Do not bear false witness, Defraud not, Honour thy father and mother.
20 And he answered and said unto him, Master, all these have I observed from my youth.
21 Then Jesus beholding him loved him, and said unto him, One thing thou lackest: go thy way, sell whatsoever thou hast, and give to the poor, and thou shalt have treasure in heaven: and come, take up the cross, and follow me.
22 And he was sad at that saying, and went away grieved: for he had great possessions.
23 And Jesus looked round about, and saith unto his disciples, How hardly shall they that have riches enter into the kingdom of God!
24 And the disciples were astonished at his words. But Jesus answereth again, and saith unto them, Children, how hard is it for them that trust in riches to enter into the kingdom of God!
25 It is easier for a camel to go through the eye of a needle, than for a rich man to enter into the kingdom of God.
26 And they were astonished out of measure, saying among themselves, Who then can be saved?
27 And Jesus looking upon them saith, With men it is impossible, but not with God: for with God all things are possible.
28 Then Peter began to say unto him, Lo, we have left all, and have followed thee.
29 And Jesus answered and said, Verily I say unto you, There is no man that hath left house, or brethren, or sisters, or father, or mother, or wife, or children, or lands, for my sake, and the gospel's,
30 But he shall receive an hundredfold now in this time, houses, and brethren, and sisters, and mothers, and children, and lands, with persecutions; and in the world to come eternal life.
31 But many that are first shall be last; and the last first.
32 And they were in the way going up to Jerusalem; and Jesus went before them: and they were amazed; and as they followed, they were afraid. And he took again the twelve, and began to tell them what things should happen unto him,
33 Saying, Behold, we go up to Jerusalem; and the Son of man shall be delivered unto the chief priests, and unto the scribes; and they shall condemn him to death, and shall deliver him to the Gentiles:
34 And they shall mock him, and shall scourge him, and shall spit upon him, and shall kill him: and the third day he shall rise again.

35 And James and John, the sons of Zebedee, come unto him, saying, Master, we would that thou shouldest do for us whatsoever we shall desire.

36 And he said unto them, What would ye that I should do for you?

37 They said unto him, Grant unto us that we may sit, one on thy right hand, and the other on thy left hand, in thy glory.

38 But Jesus said unto them, Ye know not what ye ask: can ye drink of the cup that I drink of? and be baptized with the baptism that I am baptized with?

39 And they said unto him, We can. And Jesus said unto them, Ye shall indeed drink of the cup that I drink of; and with the baptism that I am baptized withal shall ye be baptized:

40 But to sit on my right hand and on my left hand is not mine to give; but it shall be given to them for whom it is prepared.

41 And when the ten heard it, they began to be much displeased with James and John.

42 But Jesus called them to him, and saith unto them, Ye know that they which are accounted to rule over the Gentiles exercise lordship over them; and their great ones exercise authority upon them.

43 But so shall it not be among you: but whosoever will be great among you, shall be your minister:

44 And whosoever of you will be the chiefest, shall be servant of all.

45 For even the Son of man came not to be ministered unto, but to minister, and to give his life a ransom for many.

46 And they came to Jericho: and as he went out of Jericho with his disciples and a great number of people, blind Bartimaeus, the son of Timaeus, sat by the highway side begging.

47 And when he heard that it was Jesus of Nazareth, he began to cry out, and say, Jesus, thou son of David, have mercy on me.

48 And many charged him that he should hold his peace: but he cried the more a great deal, Thou son of David, have mercy on me.

49 And Jesus stood still, and commanded him to be called. And they call the blind man, saying unto him, Be of good comfort, rise; he calleth thee.

50 And he, casting away his garment, rose, and came to Jesus.

51 And Jesus answered and said unto him, What wilt thou that I should do unto thee? The blind man said unto him, Lord, that I might receive my sight.

52 And Jesus said unto him, Go thy way; thy faith hath

years before in the Old Testament. Christ felt the rejection of the people, the pain of the Roman lash and hammer, and the ridicule of the spitting and the mockery; but nothing would stop Him from dying for the world. This verse shows us God's love and man's wickedness.

10.38 The "baptism" the Lord Jesus spoke of referred to His suffering and death. (Luke 12.50).

10.39 James and John would also drink of the cup of suffering before they entered the glory of Heaven. James would be martyred and John exiled for Christ (see Acts 12.2 and Revelation 1.9).

10.44 This is very similar teaching to 9.34-37. The political world may have its hierarchy of power, but that is not to be seen amongst the disciples. He, the greatest of men, had come to serve and give His life.

10.45 "Ransom" - the price to release us from the captivity of sin and Satan was the blood of Christ.

10.48 This man was determined that the crowd would not prevent him from finding Christ, and as a result he was blessed. The crowd will always try to deter us from receiving God's salvation.

10.49 The Lord Jesus never passes anyone who cries for mercy.

10.52 After he was healed he followed Jesus in the way of truth (see John 14.6).

11.3 The "Lord" not 'Jesus of Nazareth' is His title here! As 'Lord' He has all authority and supremacy. The disciples had acknowledged Him as Lord of their life - have you?

11.10 This was all a fulfillment of Old Testament prophecy (see Zechariah 9.9).

11.13 Often figs were left from a previous harvest. The leaves raised the hope of fruit but this hope was dashed. This fig tree was a picture of Israel, God's nation, who gave the impression of being a holy people, but in reality they offered nothing to God (see vv.14-15). God's blessing today is not limited to a nation but is open for the whole world.

11.15 The temple of God had become a place for money making. The Lord Jesus would not tolerate the place of God's Name to be corrupted by commerce.

made thee whole. And immediately he received his sight, and followed Jesus in the way.

Mark 11

1 And when they came nigh to Jerusalem, unto Bethphage and Bethany, at the mount of Olives, he sendeth forth two of his disciples,
2 And saith unto them, Go your way into the village over against you: and as soon as ye be entered into it, ye shall find a colt tied, whereon never man sat; loose him, and bring him.
3 And if any man say unto you, Why do ye this? say ye that the Lord hath need of him; and straightway he will send him hither.
4 And they went their way, and found the colt tied by the door without in a place where two ways met; and they loose him.
5 And certain of them that stood there said unto them, What do ye, loosing the colt?
6 And they said unto them even as Jesus had commanded: and they let them go.
7 And they brought the colt to Jesus, and cast their garments on him; and he sat upon him.
8 And many spread their garments in the way: and others cut down branches off the trees, and strawed them in the way.
9 And they that went before, and they that followed, cried, saying, Hosanna; Blessed is he that cometh in the name of the Lord:
10 Blessed be the kingdom of our father David, that cometh in the name of the Lord: Hosanna in the highest.
11 And Jesus entered into Jerusalem, and into the temple: and when he had looked round about upon all things, and now the eventide was come, he went out unto Bethany with the twelve.
12 And on the morrow, when they were come from Bethany, he was hungry:
13 And seeing a fig tree afar off having leaves, he came, if haply he might find any thing thereon: and when he came to it, he found nothing but leaves; for the time of figs was not yet.
14 And Jesus answered and said unto it, No man eat fruit of thee hereafter for ever. And his disciples heard it.
15 And they come to Jerusalem: and Jesus went into the temple, and began to cast out them that sold and bought in the temple, and overthrew the tables of the moneychangers, and the seats of them that sold doves;
16 And would not suffer that any man should carry any

vessel through the temple.

17 And he taught, saying unto them, Is it not written, My house shall be called of all nations the house of prayer? but ye have made it a den of thieves.

18 And the scribes and chief priests heard it, and sought how they might destroy him: for they feared him, because all the people was astonished at his doctrine.

19 And when even was come, he went out of the city.

20 And in the morning, as they passed by, they saw the fig tree dried up from the roots.

21 And Peter calling to remembrance saith unto him, Master, behold, the fig tree which thou cursedst is withered away.

22 And Jesus answering saith unto them, Have faith in God.

23 For verily I say unto you, That whosoever shall say unto this mountain, Be thou removed, and be thou cast into the sea; and shall not doubt in his heart, but shall believe that those things which he saith shall come to pass; he shall have whatsoever he saith.

24 Therefore I say unto you, What things soever ye desire, when ye pray, believe that ye receive them, and ye shall have them.

25 And when ye stand praying, forgive, if ye have ought against any: that your Father also which is in heaven may forgive you your trespasses.

26 But if ye do not forgive, neither will your Father which is in heaven forgive your trespasses.

27 And they come again to Jerusalem: and as he was walking in the temple, there come to him the chief priests, and the scribes, and the elders,

28 And say unto him, By what authority doest thou these things? and who gave thee this authority to do these things?

29 And Jesus answered and said unto them, I will also ask of you one question, and answer me, and I will tell you by what authority I do these things.

30 The baptism of John, was it from heaven, or of men? answer me.

31 And they reasoned with themselves, saying, If we shall say, From heaven; he will say, Why then did ye not believe him?

32 But if we shall say, Of men; they feared the people: for all men counted John, that he was a prophet indeed.

33 And they answered and said unto Jesus, We cannot tell. And Jesus answering saith unto them, Neither do I tell you by what authority I do these things.

11.21 See verse 13-14. The withered fig tree was an object lesson of the spiritual demise of the nation of Israel.

11.24 "When ye pray, believe". True prayer is always done in faith.

11.30 The Lord Jesus displays His authority in verses 15 to 17 - He is the Son of God. However, in order to show the unbelief and insincerity of the questioners' hearts, He asked a counter question about John the Baptist.

Mark 12

12.1-6 The vineyard is God's heritage in Israel; the husbandmen are the leaders of the people of Israel; the servants are prophets whom God sent to Israel; the Son is the Lord Jesus whom they rejected and crucified.

12.6 God had only one Son and yet He gave Him to die for this wicked world.

12.10 The scripture is Psalm 118.22.

12.12 The truth hurts! The Jews knew this was true. They did indeed want to kill Him.

12.14 This was a loaded question. They thought that it was impossible for Him to answer it. To criticise Caesar would be to annoy the Herodians, and to compliment Caesar would enrage the Pharisees. However, the Lord Jesus would never allow politics or nationalism to hinder the truth. As always, He answers their question with infinite wisdom.

1 And he began to speak unto them by parables. A certain man planted a vineyard, and set an hedge about it, and digged a place for the winefat, and built a tower, and let it out to husbandmen, and went into a far country.
2 And at the season he sent to the husbandmen a servant, that he might receive from the husbandmen of the fruit of the vineyard.
3 And they caught him, and beat him, and sent him away empty.
4 And again he sent unto them another servant; and at him they cast stones, and wounded him in the head, and sent him away shamefully handled.
5 And again he sent another; and him they killed, and many others; beating some, and killing some.
6 Having yet therefore one son, his wellbeloved, he sent him also last unto them, saying, They will reverence my son.
7 But those husbandmen said among themselves, This is the heir; come, let us kill him, and the inheritance shall be ours.'
8 And they took him, and killed him, and cast him out of the vineyard.
9 What shall therefore the lord of the vineyard do? he will come and destroy the husbandmen, and will give the vineyard unto others.
10 And have ye not read this scripture; The stone which the builders rejected is become the head of the corner:
11 This was the Lord's doing, and it is marvellous in our eyes?
12 And they sought to lay hold on him, but feared the people: for they knew that he had spoken the parable against them: and they left him, and went their way.
13 And they send unto him certain of the Pharisees and of the Herodians, to catch him in his words.
14 And when they were come, they say unto him, Master, we know that thou art true, and carest for no man: for thou regardest not the person of men, but teachest the way of God in truth: Is it lawful to give tribute to Caesar, or not?
15 Shall we give, or shall we not give? But he, knowing their hypocrisy, said unto them, Why tempt ye me? bring me a penny, that I may see it.
16 And they brought it. And he saith unto them, Whose is this image and superscription? And they said unto him, Caesar's.
17 And Jesus answering said unto them, Render to Caesar the things that are Caesar's, and to God the things that are God's. And they marvelled at him.
18 Then come unto him the Sadducees, which say there

is no resurrection; and they asked him, saying,

19 Master, Moses wrote unto us, If a man's brother die, and leave his wife behind him, and leave no children, that his brother should take his wife, and raise up seed unto his brother.

20 Now there were seven brethren: and the first took a wife, and dying left no seed.

21 And the second took her, and died, neither left he any seed: and the third likewise.

22 And the seven had her, and left no seed: last of all the woman died also.

23 In the resurrection therefore, when they shall rise, whose wife shall she be of them? for the seven had her to wife.

24 And Jesus answering said unto them, Do ye not therefore err, because ye know not the scriptures, neither the power of God?

25 For when they shall rise from the dead, they neither marry, nor are given in marriage; but are as the angels which are in heaven.

26 And as touching the dead, that they rise: have ye not read in the book of Moses, how in the bush God spake unto him, saying, I am the God of Abraham, and the God of Isaac, and the God of Jacob?

27 He is not the God of the dead, but the God of the living: ye therefore do greatly err.

28 And one of the scribes came, and having heard them reasoning together, and perceiving that he had answered them well, asked him, Which is the first commandment of all?

29 And Jesus answered him, The first of all the commandments is, Hear, O Israel; The Lord our God is one Lord:

30 And thou shalt love the Lord thy God with all thy heart, and with all thy soul, and with all thy mind, and with all thy strength: this is the first commandment.

31 And the second is like, namely this, Thou shalt love thy neighbour as thyself. There is none other commandment greater than these.

32 And the scribe said unto him, Well, Master, thou hast said the truth: for there is one God; and there is none other but he:

33 And to love him with all the heart, and with all the understanding, and with all the soul, and with all the strength, and to love his neighbour as himself, is more than all whole burnt offerings and sacrifices.

34 And when Jesus saw that he answered discreetly, he said unto him, Thou art not far from the kingdom of God. And no man after that durst ask him any question.

35 And Jesus answered and said, while he taught in the

12.19 This is a reference to the ancient practice of levirate marriage in the book of Deuteronomy (25.5-10). This law preserved a family name and inheritance from disappearing.

12.24 If these men had known the Scriptures they would have understood that family relationships do not continue in Heaven. How sad when supposed 'spiritual' leaders neither know their Bible nor believe in resurrection (v.18).

12.26. The Lord teaches a wonderful truth from a present tense. He does not say "I was" but "I AM". He is still the God of Abraham. Abraham is awaiting the day when his soul will be reunited with a resurrected body.

12.34 "Discreetly" means "intelligently". The Scribe knew that religious services (sacrifices) were less important than a man having a deep love for God and his neighbour. He was not far from the kingdom, but to enter in he would have to realise that no man's heart was perfect in the sight of God, and only by the kindness and forgiveness of God can anyone enter God's kingdom.

12.37 The Lord is teaching from Psalm 110 that He existed long before king David; that He was, in fact, David's Lord. He was also David's son in the sense that He was born into this world as a man whose lineage, through His earthly guardian Joseph, could be traced back to David (see Matthew 1 vv.1-17).

12.44 The humility and sacrificial offering of the widow is commended in contrast to the boastful, yet meagre giving of the people.

13.2 The Lord Jesus was foretelling the fall and desecration of Jerusalem in AD 70 by the Romans. He was also telling His disciples not to be impressed with the physical and tangible world, which does not last, but instead, to hold on to the unseen and eternal things, which last forever. He then began to speak about the terrible events that will precede His future kingdom, which is eternal.

temple, How say the scribes that Christ is the son of David?

36 For David himself said by the Holy Ghost, The Lord said to my Lord, Sit thou on my right hand, till I make thine enemies thy footstool.

37 David therefore himself calleth him Lord; and whence is he then his son? And the common people heard him gladly.

38 And he said unto them in his doctrine, Beware of the scribes, which love to go in long clothing, and love salutations in the marketplaces,

39 And the chief seats in the synagogues, and the uppermost rooms at feasts:

40 Which devour widows' houses, and for a pretence make long prayers: these shall receive greater damnation.

41 And Jesus sat over against the treasury, and beheld how the people cast money into the treasury: and many that were rich cast in much.

42 And there came a certain poor widow, and she threw in two mites, which make a farthing.

43 And he called unto him his disciples, and saith unto them, Verily I say unto you, That this poor widow hath cast more in, than all they which have cast into the treasury:

44 For all they did cast in of their abundance; but she of her want did cast in all that she had, even all her living.

Mark 13

1 And as he went out of the temple, one of his disciples saith unto him, Master, see what manner of stones and what buildings are here!

2 And Jesus answering said unto him, Seest thou these great buildings? there shall not be left one stone upon another, that shall not be thrown down.

3 And as he sat upon the mount of Olives over against the temple, Peter and James and John and Andrew asked him privately,

4 Tell us, when shall these things be? and what shall be the sign when all these things shall be fulfilled?

5 And Jesus answering them began to say, Take heed lest any man deceive you:

6 For many shall come in my name, saying, I am Christ; and shall deceive many.

7 And when ye shall hear of wars and rumours of wars, be ye not troubled: for such things must needs be; but the end shall not be yet.

8 For nation shall rise against nation, and kingdom against kingdom: and there shall be earthquakes in divers places,

and there shall be famines and troubles: these are the beginnings of sorrows.

9 But take heed to yourselves: for they shall deliver you up to councils; and in the synagogues ye shall be beaten: and ye shall be brought before rulers and kings for my sake, for a testimony against them.

10 And the gospel must first be published among all nations.

11 But when they shall lead you, and deliver you up, take no thought beforehand what ye shall speak, neither do ye premeditate: but whatsoever shall be given you in that hour, that speak ye: for it is not ye that speak, but the Holy Ghost.

12 Now the brother shall betray the brother to death, and the father the son; and children shall rise up against their parents, and shall cause them to be put to death.

13 And ye shall be hated of all men for my name's sake: but he that shall endure unto the end, the same shall be saved.

14 But when ye shall see the abomination of desolation, spoken of by Daniel the prophet, standing where it ought not, (let him that readeth understand,) then let them that be in Judaea flee to the mountains:

15 And let him that is on the housetop not go down into the house, neither enter therein, to take any thing out of his house:

16 And let him that is in the field not turn back again for to take up his garment.

17 But woe to them that are with child, and to them that give suck in those days!

18 And pray ye that your flight be not in the winter.

19 For in those days shall be affliction, such as was not from the beginning of the creation which God created unto this time, neither shall be.

20 And except that the Lord had shortened those days, no flesh should be saved: but for the elect's sake, whom he hath chosen, he hath shortened the days.

21 And then if any man shall say to you, Lo, here is Christ; or, lo, he is there; believe him not:

22 For false Christs and false prophets shall rise, and shall shew signs and wonders, to seduce, if it were possible, even the elect.

23 But take ye heed: behold, I have foretold you all things.

24 But in those days, after that tribulation, the sun shall be darkened, and the moon shall not give her light,

25 And the stars of heaven shall fall, and the powers that are in heaven shall be shaken.

26 And then shall they see the Son of man coming in the clouds with great power and glory.

13.12 The Lord Jesus was announcing that the sin of the world would become so bad that families will be encouraged to expose family members who are Christians and turn them over to the authorities to be executed. In certain countries such happenings are being carried out even today.

13.14 The book of Daniel speaks about "the abomination of desolation" (Daniel 9.27). The antichrist will hold tremendous power worldwide. He will break his pact with the Jews and stand in the temple in Jerusalem claiming to be God (2 Thessalonians 2.3-4). These events will follow shortly after Christ's return for the church (the next prophetical event to take place) and before Christ's appearing to the world as the true Messiah (1 Thess.4.13-18; 2Thess.2.1- 9).

13.20 The next event in God's calendar is the return of Christ to the air for all believers (1 Thessalonians 4.16-17). Shortly after this the persecution will commence. Christ will return again to the earth after the tribulation to judge and to reign. It is this persecution and subsequent return of Christ to the earth that is the context of this chapter.

13.23 Nothing can thwart the plans of God. Nothing can take Him by surprise.

13.25 Stellar activity in the heavens will be a significant sign that the Lord Jesus is coming back to earth in judgement.

27 And then shall he send his angels, and shall gather together his elect from the four winds, from the uttermost part of the earth to the uttermost part of heaven.
28 Now learn a parable of the fig tree; When her branch is yet tender, and putteth forth leaves, ye know that summer is near:
29 So ye in like manner, when ye shall see these things come to pass, know that it is nigh, even at the doors.
30 Verily I say unto you, that this generation shall not pass, till all these things be done.

13.31 His "words" not 'His word'. It is not just the general message of the Saviour that is eternal but every word He said!

31 Heaven and earth shall pass away: but my words shall not pass away.
32 But of that day and that hour knoweth no man, no, not the angels which are in heaven, neither the Son, but the Father.
33 Take ye heed, watch and pray: for ye know not when the time is.
34 For the Son of Man is as a man taking a far journey, who left his house, and gave authority to his servants, and to every man his work, and commanded the porter to watch.

13.37 The Lord Jesus is saying that when He does come back it will be sudden (see comments for 13.20). Are you ready?

35 Watch ye therefore: for ye know not when the master of the house cometh, at even, or at midnight, or at the cockcrowing, or in the morning:
36 Lest coming suddenly he find you sleeping.
37 And what I say unto you I say unto all, Watch.

Mark 14

14.1 The Passover was a seven-day Jewish festival celebrating the time that they had been liberated as slaves from Egypt on Passover night (Exodus 12). The Jews still celebrate it today but fail to see that the Lord Jesus became the 'true Passover' (1 Cor. 5.7) when He died for sin to liberate us from sin's power and punishment.

1 After two days was the feast of the passover, and of unleavened bread: and the chief priests and the scribes sought how they might take him by craft, and put him to death.
2 But they said, Not on the feast day, lest there be an uproar of the people.
3 And being in Bethany in the house of Simon the leper, as he sat at meat, there came a woman having an alabaster box of ointment of spikenard very precious; and she brake the box, and poured it on his head.
4 And there were some that had indignation within themselves, and said, Why was this waste of the ointment made?

14.5 "three hundred pence" – very costly, almost an annual salary for a working man.

5 For it might have been sold for more than three hundred pence, and have been given to the poor. And they murmured against her.
6 And Jesus said, Let her alone; why trouble ye her? she hath wrought a good work on me.
7 For ye have the poor with you always, and whensoever ye will ye may do them good: but me ye have not always.

8 She hath done what she could: she is come aforehand to anoint my body to the burying.

9 Verily I say unto you, Wheresoever this gospel shall be preached throughout the whole world, this also that she hath done shall be spoken of for a memorial of her.

10 And Judas Iscariot, one of the twelve, went unto the chief priests, to betray him unto them.

11 And when they heard it, they were glad, and promised to give him money. And he sought how he might conveniently betray him.

12 And the first day of unleavened bread, when they killed the passover, his disciples said unto him, Where wilt thou that we go and prepare that thou mayest eat the passover?

13 And he sendeth forth two of his disciples, and saith unto them, Go ye into the city, and there shall meet you a man bearing a pitcher of water: follow him.

14 And wheresoever he shall go in, say ye to the goodman of the house, The Master saith, Where is the guestchamber, where I shall eat the passover with my disciples?

15 And he will shew you a large upper room furnished and prepared: there make ready for us.

16 And his disciples went forth, and came into the city, and found as he had said unto them: and they made ready the passover.

17 And in the evening he cometh with the twelve.

18 And as they sat and did eat, Jesus said, Verily I say unto you, One of you which eateth with me shall betray me.

19 And they began to be sorrowful, and to say unto him one by one, Is it I? and another said, Is it I?

20 And he answered and said unto them, It is one of the twelve, that dippeth with me in the dish.

21 The Son of man indeed goeth, as it is written of him: but woe to that man by whom the Son of man is betrayed! good were it for that man if he had never been born.

22 And as they did eat, Jesus took bread, and blessed, and brake it, and gave to them, and said, Take, eat: this is my body.

23 And he took the cup, and when he had given thanks, he gave it to them: and they all drank of it.

24 And he said unto them, This is my blood of the new testament, which is shed for many.

25 Verily I say unto you, I will drink no more of the fruit of the vine, until that day that I drink it new in the kingdom of God.

26 And when they had sung an hymn, they went out into the mount of Olives.

27 And Jesus saith unto them, All ye shall be offended because of me this night: for it is written, I will smite the shepherd, and the sheep shall be scattered.

14.8 This woman perceived what the others did not. She realised that the Lord Jesus was to die outside Jerusalem. Rather than embalming His body with the ointment after His death, she took the opportunity to do it during His life! Have we grasped our opportunity to please God by placing our trust in His Son while we still have the chance?

14.22 Many Christians today meet on the first day of the week (Sunday) to remember their Lord as He requested (see Luke 22.19; Acts 20.7).

14.25 The Lord Jesus looked beyond the Cross to His ascension to Heaven to be with His Father. Before this was possible He had to accomplish the task of putting away sin by offering His life as a ransom upon the Cross.

14.28 The Lord Jesus foretold His resurrection as early as 8.31. Now He is foretelling where He will meet the disciples after His resurrection.

14.33 "Sore amazed" means "very distressed".

14.36 The Lord Jesus knew that He would not only suffer at the hands of men, but that He would also be punished by His Father for the sin of the world. Being holy Himself, the anticipation of this suffering filled Him with deep sorrow. However, He wanted to do His Father's will, and a very vital part of that would entail suffering on account of sinners.

14.40 "Wist" means "knew"

14.46 The Lord offered no resistance. He accepted the betraying kiss of Judas, and allowed men to do their worst to Him in order that God's purposes would be fulfilled.

28 But after that I am risen, I will go before you into Galilee.
29 But Peter said unto him, Although all shall be offended, yet will not I.
30 And Jesus saith unto him, Verily I say unto thee, That this day, even in this night, before the cock crow twice, thou shalt deny me thrice.
31 But he spake the more vehemently, If I should die with thee, I will not deny thee in any wise. Likewise also said they all.
32 And they came to a place which was named Gethsemane: and he saith to his disciples, Sit ye here, while I shall pray.
33 And he taketh with him Peter and James and John, and began to be sore amazed, and to be very heavy;
34 And saith unto them, My soul is exceeding sorrowful unto death: tarry ye here, and watch.
35 And he went forward a little, and fell on the ground, and prayed that, if it were possible, the hour might pass from him.
36 And he said, Abba, Father, all things are possible unto thee; take away this cup from me: nevertheless not what I will, but what thou wilt.
37 And he cometh, and findeth them sleeping, and saith unto Peter, Simon, sleepest thou? couldest not thou watch one hour?
38 Watch ye and pray, lest ye enter into temptation. The spirit truly is ready, but the flesh is weak.
39 And again he went away, and prayed, and spake the same words.
40 And when he returned, he found them asleep again, (for their eyes were heavy,) neither wist they what to answer him.
41 And he cometh the third time, and saith unto them, Sleep on now, and take your rest: it is enough, the hour is come; behold, the Son of man is betrayed into the hands of sinners.
42 Rise up, let us go; lo, he that betrayeth me is at hand.
43 And immediately, while he yet spake, cometh Judas, one of the twelve, and with him a great multitude with swords and staves, from the chief priests and the scribes and the elders.
44 And he that betrayed him had given them a token, saying, Whomsoever I shall kiss, that same is he; take him, and lead him away safely.
45 And as soon as he was come, he goeth straightway to him, and saith, Master, master; and kissed him.
46 And they laid their hands on him, and took him.
47 And one of them that stood by drew a sword, and smote a servant of the high priest, and cut off his ear.
48 And Jesus answered and said unto them, Are ye come

out, as against a thief, with swords and with staves to take me?

49 I was daily with you in the temple teaching, and ye took me not: but the scriptures must be fulfilled.

50 And they all forsook him, and fled.

51 And there followed him a certain young man, having a linen cloth cast about his naked body; and the young men laid hold on him:

52 And he left the linen cloth, and fled from them naked.

53 And they led Jesus away to the high priest: and with him were assembled all the chief priests and the elders and the scribes.

54 And Peter followed him afar off, even into the palace of the high priest: and he sat with the servants, and warmed himself at the fire.

55 And the chief priests and all the council sought for witness against Jesus to put him to death; and found none.

56 For many bare false witness against him, but their witness agreed not together.

57 And there arose certain, and bare false witness against him, saying,

58 We heard him say, I will destroy this temple that is made with hands, and within three days I will build another made without hands.

59 But neither so did their witness agree together.

60 And the high priest stood up in the midst, and asked Jesus, saying, Answerest thou nothing? what is it which these witness against thee?

61 But he held his peace, and answered nothing. Again the high priest asked him, and said unto him, Art thou the Christ, the Son of the Blessed?

62 And Jesus said, I am: and ye shall see the Son of man sitting on the right hand of power, and coming in the clouds of heaven.

63 Then the high priest rent his clothes, and saith, What need we any further witnesses?

64 Ye have heard the blasphemy: what think ye? And they all condemned him to be guilty of death.

65 And some began to spit on him, and to cover his face, and to buffet him, and to say unto him, Prophesy: and the servants did strike him with the palms of their hands.

66 And as Peter was beneath in the palace, there cometh one of the maids of the high priest:

67 And when she saw Peter warming himself, she looked upon him, and said, And thou also wast with Jesus of Nazareth.

68 But he denied, saying, I know not, neither understand I what thou sayest. And he went out into the porch; and

14.49 The Old Testament Scriptures foretell all of these events e.g. Judas' betrayal, Psalm 41.9. and the Crucifixion Psalm 22.16.

14.51 Many have wondered if this is Mark himself.

14.56 No corroborated evidence could be found against Christ (see v.59).

14.58 Read John 2.19-22. The Lord Jesus was speaking of his body in resurrection- not Herod's temple.

14.61 The real charge against the Lord Jesus was that He claimed to be the Messiah - the King of the world, the Son of God. Their problem was not with what He had done (for He was righteous) but the claims He had made regarding His deity (see 15.10).

the cock crew.

69 And a maid saw him again, and began to say to them that stood by, This is one of them.

70 And he denied it again. And a little after, they that stood by said again to Peter, Surely thou art one of them: for thou art a Galilaean, and thy speech agreeth thereto.

71 But he began to curse and to swear, saying, I know not this man of whom ye speak.

72 And the second time the cock crew. And Peter called to mind the word that Jesus said unto him, Before the cock crow twice, thou shalt deny me thrice. And when he thought thereon, he wept.

14.72 Christians can fail. Peter feared the crowd and acted out of character. But he still loved the Lord, as testified by his tears.

Mark 15

1 And straightway in the morning the chief priests held a consultation with the elders and scribes and the whole council, and bound Jesus, and carried him away, and delivered him to Pilate.

2 And Pilate asked him, Art thou the King of the Jews? And he answering said unto them, Thou sayest it.

3 And the chief priests accused him of many things: but he answered nothing.

4 And Pilate asked him again, saying, Answerest thou nothing? behold how many things they witness against thee.

5 But Jesus yet answered nothing; so that Pilate marvelled.

6 Now at that feast he released unto them one prisoner, whomsoever they desired.

7 And there was one named Barabbas, which lay bound with them that had made insurrection with him, who had committed murder in the insurrection.

8 And the multitude crying aloud began to desire him to do as he had ever done unto them.

9 But Pilate answered them, saying, Will ye that I release unto you the King of the Jews?

10 For he knew that the chief priests had delivered him for envy.

11 But the chief priests moved the people, that he should rather release Barabbas unto them.

12 And Pilate answered and said again unto them, What will ye then that I shall do unto him whom ye call the King of the Jews?

13 And they cried out again, Crucify him.

14 Then Pilate said unto them, Why, what evil hath he done? And they cried out the more exceedingly, Crucify him.

15 And so Pilate, willing to content the people, released

5.2 The expression "thou sayest" is an expression confirming the truth of what has been said. Translate, "It is as you say".

15.11 Barabbas or Christ? All of us are faced with the same question. Will Christ have the central place in our life or someone/something else?

Barabbas unto them, and delivered Jesus, when he had scourged him, to be crucified.

16 And the soldiers led him away into the hall, called Praetorium; and they call together the whole band.

17 And they clothed him with purple, and platted a crown of thorns, and put it about his head,

18 And began to salute him, Hail, King of the Jews!

19 And they smote him on the head with a reed, and did spit upon him, and bowing their knees worshipped him.

20 And when they had mocked him, they took off the purple from him, and put his own clothes on him, and led him out to crucify him.

21 And they compel one Simon a Cyrenian, who passed by, coming out of the country, the father of Alexander and Rufus, to bear his cross.

22 And they bring him unto the place Golgotha, which is, being interpreted, The place of a skull.

23 And they gave him to drink wine mingled with myrrh: but he received it not.

24 And when they had crucified him, they parted his garments, casting lots upon them, what every man should take.

25 And it was the third hour, and they crucified him.

26 And the superscription of his accusation was written over, The King Of The Jews.

27 And with him they crucify two thieves; the one on his right hand, and the other on his left.

28 And the scripture was fulfilled, which saith, And he was numbered with the transgressors.

29 And they that passed by railed on him, wagging their heads, and saying, Ah, thou that destroyest the temple, and buildest it in three days,

30 Save thyself, and come down from the cross.

31 Likewise also the chief priests mocking said among themselves with the scribes, He saved others; himself he cannot save.

32 Let Christ the King of Israel descend now from the cross, that we may see and believe. And they that were crucified with him reviled him.

33 And when the sixth hour was come, there was darkness over the whole land until the ninth hour.

34 And at the ninth hour Jesus cried with a loud voice, saying, Eloi, Eloi, lama sabachthani? which is, being interpreted, My God, my God, why hast thou forsaken me?

35 And some of them that stood by, when they heard it, said, Behold, he calleth Elias.

36 And one ran and filled a spunge full of vinegar, and put it on a reed, and gave him to drink, saying, Let alone; let us see whether Elias will come to take him down.

15.17 Purple was the colour of royalty. They ridiculed His claim to be king. The eastern thorns, (measuring approx. 8cm long), were battered into His brow as a mock crown. Yet the One who had the authority to banish all to Hell, never responded in insult or hatred.

15.22 A skull shaped hill outside Jerusalem, also called Calvary.

15.28 The Scripture referred to here is Isaiah 53.12.

15.32 This ridicule was of the devil himself. Of course the Lord could have come down from the Cross, but if He had, there would be no salvation from the curse and penalty of our sin! Sin could only be put away by the sacrifice of Christ's life on the cross.

15.33-34 These three hours of darkness were the most important point of time in the history of the world. It was then that God punished His Son for the sins of the world. The punishment that all men and women rightly deserve was borne by Christ. God could now pardon sin and still be righteous, as sin was now dealt with in the death of His perfect Son (Romans 3.24-26) .

15.37 The loud cry of the Lord Jesus on the Cross shows us that this was no ordinary death - He went into death voluntarily, for death had no claim on Him (see v.44).

15.38 The veil in the temple separated the 'most holy place' from the rest of the temple. The fact that it was torn in two and from the top to the bottom shows that God has finished with the temple system of religion. A relationship with God is now possible, not through the Jewish religion and ordinances, but through faith in His Son.

16.1 Embalming the body of the dead was common in the east.

16.3 The issue that was causing such consternation was the size of the stone and possibly also the seal of Rome at the tomb. They need not have worried as the stone was already rolled away – not to let the Saviour out but to show that He was not there. He had risen.

16.7 See 14.28.
"and Peter" – How kind of the Lord to single out Peter to encourage him after his denial.

37 And Jesus cried with a loud voice, and gave up the ghost.

38 And the veil of the temple was rent in twain from the top to the bottom.

39 And when the centurion, which stood over against him, saw that he so cried out, and gave up the ghost, he said, Truly this man was the Son of God.

40 There were also women looking on afar off: among whom was Mary Magdalene, and Mary the mother of James the less and of Joses, and Salome;

41 (Who also, when he was in Galilee, followed him, and ministered unto him;) and many other women which came up with him unto Jerusalem.

42 And now when the even was come, because it was the preparation, that is, the day before the sabbath,

43 Joseph of Arimathaea, an honourable counsellor, which also waited for the kingdom of God, came, and went in boldly unto Pilate, and craved the body of Jesus.

44 And Pilate marvelled if he were already dead: and calling unto him the centurion, he asked him whether he had been any while dead.

45 And when he knew it of the centurion, he gave the body to Joseph.

46 And he bought fine linen, and took him down, and wrapped him in the linen, and laid him in a sepulchre which was hewn out of a rock, and rolled a stone unto the door of the sepulchre.

47 And Mary Magdalene and Mary the mother of Joses beheld where he was laid.

Mark 16

1 And when the sabbath was past, Mary Magdalene, and Mary the mother of James, and Salome, had bought sweet spices, that they might come and anoint him.

2 And very early in the morning the first day of the week, they came unto the sepulchre at the rising of the sun.

3 And they said among themselves, Who shall roll us away the stone from the door of the sepulchre?

4 And when they looked, they saw that the stone was rolled away: for it was very great.

5 And entering into the sepulchre, they saw a young man sitting on the right side, clothed in a long white garment; and they were affrighted.

6 And he saith unto them, Be not affrighted: Ye seek Jesus of Nazareth, which was crucified: he is risen; he is not here: behold the place where they laid him.

7 But go your way, tell his disciples and Peter that he goeth before you into Galilee: there shall ye see him, as he said unto you.

8 And they went out quickly, and fled from the sepulchre; for they trembled and were amazed: neither said they any thing to any man; for they were afraid.

9 Now when Jesus was risen early the first day of the week, he appeared first to Mary Magdalene, out of whom he had cast seven devils.

10 And she went and told them that had been with him, as they mourned and wept.

11 And they, when they had heard that he was alive, and had been seen of her, believed not.

12 After that he appeared in another form unto two of them, as they walked, and went into the country.

13 And they went and told it unto the residue: neither believed they them.

14 Afterward he appeared unto the eleven as they sat at meat, and upbraided them with their unbelief and hardness of heart, because they believed not them which had seen him after he was risen.

15 And he said unto them, Go ye into all the world, and preach the gospel to every creature.

16 He that believeth and is baptized shall be saved; but he that believeth not shall be damned.

17 And these signs shall follow them that believe; In my name shall they cast out devils; they shall speak with new tongues;

18 They shall take up serpents; and if they drink any deadly thing, it shall not hurt them; they shall lay hands on the sick, and they shall recover.

19 So then after the Lord had spoken unto them, he was received up into heaven, and sat on the right hand of God.

20 And they went forth, and preached every where, the Lord working with them, and confirming the word with signs following. Amen.

16.9 "He appeared". Notice the three appearings - v.12, v.14. The resurrection of Christ was a watershed. The disciples would die a martyr's death for what they had seen - a risen Saviour! This was the catalyst for the spread of Christianity. He is alive today!

16.15 The great commission from the risen Saviour was to preach the Gospel to everyone. No one is excluded.

16.17,18 In the early days of Christianity special miracles took place to demonstrate the power of the Gospel. (See Acts 3.7; 9.40; 19.11-12; 28.3-6).

16.19 The Lord Jesus is seated on the right hand of God, having finished the work that He came into the world to do. One day, very soon, He will return again (see John 14 vv.1-3). We are not told when He will return: the important thing is - are you ready if He was to return today?

EVERY DISH HAS A STORY

EVERY DISH HAS A STORY

WHEN I WAS A KID...
TREASURED CHILDHOOD
FOOD MEMORIES
AND THEIR RECIPES

JILL HECKER

NEW DEGREE PRESS

EVERY DISH HAS A STORY

When I Was a Kid...Treasured Childhood Food Memories and Their Recipes

ISBN   979-8-88504-095-2   *Paperback*

              979-8-88504-726-5   *Kindle Ebook*

              979-8-88504-205-5   *Ebook*

To my daddy, Sheldon Jay Weinberger (1931-2010),
who inspired me to appreciate food and the dining experience.
I wouldn't have discovered this astonishing
culinary world without you.

CONTENTS

——

AUTHOR'S NOTE

"I realized very early the power of food to evoke memory, to bring people together, to transport you to other places, and I wanted to be part of that."

—JOSÉ ANDRÉS PUERTA

What is your favorite food? You know, that one special delicious food that sets your heart and taste buds a-flutter. The one that you feel that child-like excitement when you know it's coming. The one that brings with it memories of the first time you ever tried it and fell in love. The one you can't wait to eat again.

Why do we look forward to these particular foods? There is a reason for that. And it almost always stems from your childhood.

Food is one of our biggest memory triggers, and we have the hippocampus to thank for that. No, that is not a new animal in the zoo; it is the part of your brain where memories are stored. Tastes and smells take you back in time to the place where you first tasted a dish and knew it was something you wanted more. It takes us back to mom's or grandma's kitchen or, in my case, some fabulous restaurants of the past.

These memories evoke happiness, love, and an overjoyed full belly.

There is a big desire for nostalgia today. Our ever-changing world yearns for the simpler times of our childhood, our comfort. It is no wonder there is a popular resurgence of the dishes of the past. Often, people fondly remember their childhood through the foods they ate as children, the family dinner table, the brown bag lunches they took to school, the after-school specials on TV they ran home as fast as they could to watch — with a snack, of course.

There is an inherent need for this. Retro-themed restaurants, bars, and parties are popping up all over the country, with people filling up booths and tables looking to transport themselves back to their childhood. We want the dinners our moms served us. We want our memories to flow back.

One of my nostalgic guilty pleasures is Taco Bell, which I allow myself on occasion — enjoying every bite along the way. As I sit in the drive-thru line, my mind wanders back to being in high school and going to Taco Bell at lunchtime. I always got the same thing, the Enchirito.

It was heaven.

A hybrid of an enchilada and a burrito with ground beef, beans, and onions rolled up in a flour tortilla, topped with their amazing red sauce, a sprinkle of cheddar cheese, and three (no more, no less) black olives. I am suddenly transported back to high school, 1981–1983, standing in line at Taco Bell talking with friends about whatever the day's gossip is, happy to be away from school.

That is what childhood memories do for us. They take us back and find smiles. Sadly, the Enchirito was discontinued in 1993. It came back for a little while in 2003 — but it was never the same. It has since been relegated to the great Taco Bell menu in the sky. Bummer.

I just have the memories, yet those memories are strong. I can see it; I can taste it. You never know when these memories will come up, and that is the fun part. Random foods come along your path in life, and all of a sudden, you are transported back to being a kid again.

My sentimentality and love of food history led me to create my YouTube channel, YesterKitchen. I wanted to share my fascination with wishes from the past along with their stories. My passion came out of a childhood where I had very few friends and became wholly withdrawn. I discovered that reading cookbooks took me to a wonderful world that blended with the food world I was introduced to by my Daddy.

I was lucky enough to be the daughter of one of the original foodies, my daddy. Was he really? Probably not. Yet, to me, he was. He was a big, strong man that loved to cook and eat. He knew all about good food, and he opened a whole world for me that set me on my own culinary path that is lasting a lifetime. From an early age, I was fortunate enough to be taken to the best restaurants Los Angeles had to offer.

One of my all-time favorites is Lawry's the Prime Rib in Beverly Hills, California, the best prime rib in the world, in my humblest of opinions. It opened in 1938 and is still in existence to this day. If you have ever heard of Lawry's Seasoned Salt, this is the same place. In fact, it was initially created in 1938 to season their prime rib and is still popular today. I will elaborate on my story of Lawry's further and also share one of their famous recipes in a secret bonus chapter at the end of the book.

Looking back at my life history, I had no idea at the time that these experiences through food were leading me to a lifelong passion for sharing our culinary past.

The more fascinated I became with the many recipes I encountered, the more I wondered where these dishes originated from. I found myself at the library, glued to books, looking up the meals I was finding in cookbooks.

Fortyish years later, I am still studying the exquisite dishes of the past and sharing them every week on my channel. It is who I am. I now refer to myself as a culinary historian being fascinated with meals spanning the 1930s–1980s, many of which I had at my family dinner table. With their ever-changing foods, these decades helped me rediscover my past, bringing me joy, where I learned so much about myself.

This book is full of wonderful stories from individuals, just like you and me — people who have traced back what brings them comfort today through the foods they grew up on. We will meet chefs, moms, dads, grandparents, writers, and so many other remarkable people, all sharing their stories about the one dish that brings them back to their childhood. When reading the stories, think of your own childhood and the foods you've experienced; you may be surprised as to what memories come back.

These stories are for everyone. Even if you don't consider yourself a foodie, there are stories within these pages that will connect to anyone and spark your own food memories. We were all children once, growing up with unique families and cultures that created meals that have a lasting impact on us. Get your nostalgia on and take a walk down memory lane. You will find yourself cooking the dishes of your past or finding restaurants serving them. Over the course of this book, you will find smiles, happiness, and inspiration.

The world needs something happy to read, and it doesn't get any happier than childhood memories through food. Your hippocampus and stomach are waiting for you.

YOU REALLY ARE WHAT YOU EAT (OR ATE), AT LEAST YOUR MIND THINKS SO

———

"Let food be thy medicine and medicine be thy food."

—HIPPOCRATES

The foods we eat as children have a profound effect on us as adults. The brain is a miraculous thing. Going into the writing of this book, I had a theory that what your food experiences were as a child, good or bad, directly reflects who you are as an adult. As it turns out, my theory was true.

I had the wonderful opportunity to interview my dear friend, Dr. Kim Perkins, on this very subject. Her PhD is in Positive Psychology. She explained some of her research to me on this fascinating topic, and what I learned from her was compelling. What we ate as children and how we were raised truly does affect who we are as adults. Who we are as adults and what we eat truly does start with our childhood and how we were raised.

For example, if family dinners were a positive time of fun, laughter, stories about the day, and good food, a child will typically grow up to embrace family dinners when they become a parent. Food was warmth; food was comfort. If one of mom's specialties was fried chicken and you were a child of a secure attachment, then one of your go-to comfort foods as an adult will most likely be fried chicken. It brings positive emotions and secure feelings every time you think of it or smell it, and you will enjoy eating it. You may even spend time trying to duplicate your mom's recipe or be on a search for the fried chicken restaurant that best creates that special flavor. The warmth and security these foods brought stays with you throughout your life, and directly reflects your feelings and actions around food. They take you back to your childhood — and you love going back.

A friend of mine told me the story of how he and his friend got into his parent's sherry when they were ten and got very sick. To this day, he can't even stand the smell of sherry, let alone taste it. The smell of food is far more powerful than the taste. It just takes one whiff, and you want out of the room. These experiences carry a long shadow.

When it comes to childhood food memories, we have such a strong reaction to something we smell, taste, or see as an adult. For instance, you may be at the market waiting to check out, and of course, those crafty markets always put all the candy bars right there while you are stuck in line. They are called impulse buys because they want you to see them, and purchase before you even give it thought. So here you are waiting in line, and all of a sudden, you see a candy bar that you loved as a kid. While you wait, you fondly remember the "good old days" and smile. You may even buy the candy and relive those memories even deeper. One bite, and you are twelve again.

According to Dr. Perkins, there are two pathways to how we process our food memories. "There is the biological one, and then there is one that is more psychological." Let's start with biological.

The limbic system is one of the oldest and most primitive parts of our brain. The various parts of the limbic system have several roles, including controlling our emotions and retaining memories. Every experience we have ever had is housed in there, including every emotion attached to everything we have ever eaten.

Within the limbic system, there are two parts that have everything to do with emotions, memories, and how we feel about foods as adults. Tucked away in the base of the brain, within the limbic system, lives the amygdala.

"Biologically speaking, the smell path, or the stimulus as we call it, gets translated into meaning in your mind." The amygdala is where our fight or flight decisions happen. It also processes positive stimuli in addition to emotional memories. In fact, scientists have not yet fully discovered everything the amygdala does.

The amygdala's decision-making is a key part of children liking some foods and not others and is completely involuntary. In simple terms, when you first taste something, the scent comes into your nose and moves on to your olfactory bulb, which is part of the front of your brain that transmits smell information from the nose to the brain. Then your brain moves it along to your limbic system. In the limbic system, your amygdala is waiting to decide if we like or dislike whatever we are tasting.

In other situations, the amygdala tells us immediately if something is a threat, and our fight or flight kicks in. Dr. Perkins shares, "It's that simple and is a snap judgement." But what is happening in your brain is very complex. Before we can even think about it, the decision is made. It's a reaction based on our experiences of the past.

When the amygdala makes its decision, our sense of smell is far more heavily weighted than the taste we receive. Something's smell gets translated into meaning via emotions in our brain, far more than its taste. "When our brain processes taste, the subtleties are really about what we are smelling," according to Dr. Perkins. "We have our basic tastes, which are sweet, salty, sour, and bitter." However, smell supersedes all of them.

You can see that for yourself if you hold your nose when you eat something, you really can't taste it.

When we were young and tried something for the first time, the amygdala immediately decided if we liked it or not—no time-lapse, no deciding, and without our input. From the amygdala's decision, the memory then goes to the hippocampus, where it gets stored for a lifetime. Dr. Perkins says, "The hippocampus is where short-term memories get stored into long-term memories. It makes it part of what you think about as being 'your story.'" This is your personal history, my friends. Your likes, your dislikes, your experiences—they are all tied to your emotions and memories. That is why smells and — to a lesser extent—tastes are so potent when it comes to our life stories.

To emphasize the role of the hippocampus, let's say you are invited to a friend's house for dinner, and they serve spaghetti and meatballs. When it's placed on the table, you can be neutral if you really don't have any specific memories attached to it. Yet, what if that was on the dinner table the night you found out your parents were getting a divorce? You may never want spaghetti and meatballs again. The hippocampus remembers the times you had it, attaches emotions, and makes all that available to you as part of your memory.

The amygdala and hippocampus also have a big role when we dine out. Many chefs take inspiration from memories of dishes their mom or grandma made, and of course, they add their chef-ey spin to take the dish to the next level. Lobster Mac and Cheese had to come from somewhere.

Besides the amygdala and hippocampus, there is also a psychological aspect to childhood food memories, Dr. Perkins shares. "This is how we as adults see food from the lens of our childhood and is called Attachment Theory." I was curious how long this theory has been around. I learned from Saul McLeod's 2017 article, "Attachment Theory," that this is a well-supported theory in the area of psychology and has been around since the 1950s.

This theory concerns the relationship between children and their caregivers, whether they be parents, grandparents, other family members, guardians, or prominent unrelated people in a child's life, such as a teacher. The relationship you have with your caregiver, good or bad, can be directly associated with the foods you like or don't like as an adult.

Interestingly, the patterns we've experienced are also what we bring with us to personal relationships as adults.

The most important pattern for this book, according to Dr. Perkins, is Secure Attachment, which means you can rely on your caregivers, you have a good relationship with them, you can depend on them, and you know they will help you. In Courtney Ackerman's 2018 article, "What is Attachment Theory? Bowlby's 4 Stages Explained," she states children will grow up to see others as supportive and helpful and themselves as competent and worthy of respect. Their outlook becomes positive; they are more successful and have more trust in others. You are able to be securely attached to someone.

The remaining three patterns are Anxious-Avoidant Attachment, Anxious Resistant Attachment, and Disorganized Attachment. These can have a negative effect on who you become, to varying degrees. Dr. Perkins elaborates, "These patterns involve varying degrees of reliance on your caregiver as a child, sometimes creating complete distrust with them. Consequently, you may learn you can only rely on yourself and can't rely on others." Unfortunately, these three patterns are not uncommon, but it can be validating and eye-opening to discover why you are the way you are as an adult.

The effects of these attachment patterns could lead to many food issues. Many adults grew up in these circumstances where they did not receive the love they needed from their caregiver. So, they turned to food, and the comfort it gave then replaced the lack of love and comfort they needed and did not receive.

As Dr. Perkins states, "These patterns can be changed, sometimes unconsciously. If you experienced some form of negative attachment and grew up in a home, for example, where fast food was a daily meal, as an adult, you may never want fast food again and adopt a healthy eating lifestyle to reverse the effects of your childhood. And you may not even know why you switched. You just now embrace vegetables and healthy eating." You may even have become a vegetarian or vegan. Or reversed, if you grew up in a vegan home and it was not a good experience, you are now a foodie loving all varieties of food. Having attachment issues could be a big reason why you eat what you do. Everyone has their own story.

What food you've experienced as a child, in whatever way, reflects who you are as an adult. Whether your comfort food takes you back to your happy childhood or your adverse one, food represents the love you felt you received. Food is comfort or the lack thereof, that is a style in and of itself. You can learn where someone came from through the foods they enjoy as an adult. As Dr. Perkins says, "Food is love."

YESTERKITCHEN'S STORY

"Food is everything we are. It's an extension of nationalist feeling, ethnic feeling, your personal history, your province, your region, your tribe, your grandma. It's inseparable from those from the get-go."

—ANTHONY BOURDAIN

My tag line is *"Every Dish has a Story,"* and I truly believe that. Every dish had a point of creation — a reason why so many people embraced it and how it became a part of someone's family. Everything we eat had to come from somewhere. These are the stories I love to tell.

When you are a young parent, you have to work hard to provide the very best life you can for your children. Between school, sports, friends, birthdays, and the many other things needed to be done when you love your children more than anything, you never stop. Then, on top of that, is your career, the job that pays the bills. Being a parent is a 24/7 job in and of itself—and the best job in the world. Then, the kids move out, and you become an empty-nester. Eventually, you come to the time when you are fortunate enough to leave corporate America. Now what?

For me, that is when I decided to ditch my fear that lasted five years and start a YouTube channel.

My foodie brain lives in the past. It's always been that way. In my forty-plus years of studying dishes popular in days gone by, I've discovered hundreds of dishes that are getting lost in history, and I am on a mission to not let that happen. The recipes need to be shared, and their stories have to be told. They are fascinating, inspiring, and surprising.

My beloved YesterKitchen. It has been my dream to share my love of retro dishes along with the stories behind them. Do you know where so many of the dishes we know and love came from? I do! But I wanted to share how I got here first.

The love of food was instilled in me for as long as I can remember. The inspiration for my passion and life's work, however, came from a very different place.

I didn't have the happiest of childhoods. It wasn't horrible by any means. I grew up in a somewhat affluent part of Los Angeles and had all I needed. Not wanted, but needed. However, I was the kid that always got teased. I know I am not alone, and for all of you that are out there that experienced similar situations, my heart goes out to you. I was very plain and somewhat overweight. My curly hair came before a time of hair products, and the result was a frizzy mess that I hated. I wore my hair in an afro for many years since hairdressers didn't know what else to do with me at the time. I was a perfect target for kids. They can be so cruel. I was called 'Brillo Head," "Bride of Frankenstein," or a myriad of other names to make a young child feel horrible. It was terrible because there was nothing I could do to change the situation. I was teased mercilessly for as long as I can remember.

Due to this, I had very few friends. I started out as any child before I ever started school, wide-eyed, excited, and happy. But, as a product of my experience in school, I became shy, withdrawn, insecure, fearful, and sad. I hated school. I hated me. I wished I were different. I wished I looked different. I wished people wanted to be my friend. I wished people didn't tease me. I wished. I wished. I wished.

Due to being so withdrawn, I started reading cookbooks when I was around ten or eleven. I would start at the first word and read the entire book. I read and reread every cookbook in my house. I went to the library and read cookbooks. It became my escape, and I immersed myself in what was becoming my passion — cooking.

Early on, I started wondering where these recipes came from. I felt such a strong curiosity and started going to the library to research the history of the dishes that captured my attention. At the time, I didn't realize the research I was doing would impact my life as much as it does. I was just escaping my reality.

I am so grateful for those cookbooks. They captured me and took me to safe and wonderful places. The history I was studying was like time travel — all-consuming.

I started going further back in time to discover more astonishing recipes. I was learning history through food which was way more fun than history in school. I learned about World War II and food rations, the Great Depression, how the 50s changed the way we cook, all those wonderful casseroles, and on and on. It was absolutely fascinating. I had no idea at the time the knowledge base I was creating. Combined with my love of cooking, I found what was to be my lifelong passion. I made some of the dishes I found in the cookbooks at home. Time has since removed which specific dishes I made from my mind. However, I remember cooking simple ones and falling in love with the act of creating food. I still have some of those very same cookbooks from my childhood and have made episodes celebrating some of the dishes.

Studying food history and cooking remained all-consuming through my lower education years. I graduated high school, and my love of cooking and food history continued to grow. Looking back, I know that I was finding happiness not in my childhood experiences but in the past through food.

College was much better. My teasing days were behind me, and I went on to earn my BA in communications. I joined the corporate world, got married, had three amazing children, got divorced, met Rod, and found true love. We have been happily married since 2007. Along with my new marriage, three wonderful stepchildren came into my life, and now my family is growing to the next generation.

Around 2013, I wanted to share my knowledge through cooking classes, yet I would be limited to reaching only a few people at a time. A friend suggested I start a YouTube channel. I immediately laughed it off. I knew a little bit about YouTube but never thought to even attempt a channel. Why? Fear. I had no clue how to start a channel. Do I even know what I am doing? What will people think of me? Will anyone even watch it? What if I look stupid? What if people I know laugh at me? What if? What if? What if?

I knew my food history, I knew how to cook, and I knew I had a concept that wasn't the average cooking channel out there. I had a special niche. My show — which I was too afraid to start at the time — would be centered on both cooking and, just as important, sharing the stories behind the dishes. But for five years, I "what if-ed" myself to death and continued to work in a corporate job that I couldn't stand, going nowhere and making myself miserable.

In 2018, my youngest son, Jason, graduated high school and was off to college. Suddenly, it was just Rod and me. That is when I got the motivation to start my channel. I was talking to one of my oldest sons, Lorenzo, and he just looked me in the eye and said, "Just start filming. You can worry about the rest later." Thank you, Lo. I am forever grateful for that. I had a huge learning curve, but so did everyone else that has ever started a channel. So, off I went.

Here is the problem as I saw it; there are fabulous classic retro dishes that are getting lost in history. These are childhood memories for so many people across the country. These special memories make them who they are today.

Current food "experts" treat classic dishes of the past as things not to be made, eaten, or even talked about. What hurts me the most is when people ridicule retro dishes as "gross." They mock the past's classics, and these classics are the roots of so much of what we eat today. You can't "update" a dish without paying homage to the original dish.

This is why I started YesterKitchen. I am on a mission to bring back retro cooking because every dish has a story, and they deserve to be told.

My favorite decades for food are the 1930s through the 1980s. Those are the ones I consider truly retro and rich in food history. Much of how we've come to know food in America and how we eat it originated from these times. We, as Americans, went through a great depression, World War II, the introduction of diners, cocktail parties, international cooking in the home, and so many other food-based events. Every decade brought new ingredients and cooking equipment with it. There was a time when refrigerators and microwaves did not exist. Kitchens were created for the "modern housewife." Many exciting changes happened, creating a magical time in food history, which I love to talk about and share. My passion is now releasing videos to bring back these stories—through the unique medium of food.

I prepared for my first episode, I had my notes, ingredients, camera set up — and I got sick. Even though I was alone in the house, I still felt like I had an audience in my kitchen. I courage-ed up and did it anyways. My first video was about Thousand Island Dressing, one of my favorite food stories, even to this day. Did you even think this dressing had a story? Yet it does, and it's interesting. If you want to see a very nervous Jill trying to make her first video, go check out that episode.

Having a YouTube channel is hard work. It requires serious dedication and love of your craft. You have grand visions about your channel taking off immediately, rarely does that happen, and that was my case. I got discouraged and wanted to quit. Very few were watching, and even fewer were subscribing. I have started many ventures in the past where I was quickly disappointed and quit. This was my absolute passion, and I wasn't going to let that happen again, so I continued on.

I was about a year into my channel and had videos covering every decade from the 1970s Cocktail Party and Cheese Fondue to World War II Food Ration Cooking and everywhere in between when I started gaining an audience. It grew very slowly — and then, momentum picked up. I was elated to know that I was not the only one that was interested in where these classic retro dishes came from. People started leaving the most surprising and kindest comments. That just warmed my heart and only encouraged me to continue.

Then, an incredible, unexpected thing happened.

Over time I started getting many comments from viewers about their childhood memories that stemmed from the dishes I happened to be presenting. I read lengthy comments sharing the stories that made them remember the dishes, and everyone started with, "I remember when my mom made that, thank you so much for sharing this! I've forgotten all about it!" These comments mainly came from the dishes of the 1960s and 1970s as those were the growing up years of most of my viewers.

It brought me joy to read comments from people sharing their lives through food memories. I was honored to be the catalyst for triggering these memories for many people. These stories were like traveling back in time to someone's home I didn't know. I was in awe that so many people were sharing their memories. I loved reading every word, and the stories continue to this day!

In 2020, I was having so much fun that I felt the need to write a book based on my channel. I wanted to expand the stories of my favorite dishes I shared on YesterKitchen. I prefer creating episodes that last around twelve minutes. However, by doing this, I have to leave out some details of the dish and story. This book was created to fill in that gap, sharing the lost stories I was not able to capture on camera. I wrote a few stories and took a break for six months; I wasn't feeling it and chose not to continue. Then I had an inspiration. It dawned on me: people love to share their personal history around why a dish is special to them through their comments. I love reading it, and I can't be alone. People are sharing a piece of their lives with each story. It's special, and it should be shared—and I was going to do just that. Thus, the new subject of this book was born. This wasn't just *my book*; this was a collection of *everyone's book*.

I sent out a request to potential interviewees and was able to lock down enough stories to create my book. I collected twenty-one interviews, and I love them all. Everyone surprised me with that one dish that brought them back to their childhood. And I hope they will surprise you too. I also hope these stories will inspire you to start thinking about the dish that brings you back to your own childhood.

When I started to write this book, I had no idea that this would become a way for me to find peace with my own childhood. Listening to other childhood stories was a healing endeavor for me, and I am grateful for every single one of them. Maybe looking back at my early years and looking at where I am now can explain that I would never be where I am without those past experiences. As painful as they were at the time, I turned out pretty well. I get to celebrate my passion that started so many years ago every day. Suppose I didn't have those experiences; who knows if I would have ever picked up a cookbook then? I had my path, and everyone else had theirs. And here we are — adults with childhood memories through food.

To those of you that generously allowed me to peek into your childhood and hear about the one dish that brought you back, thank you. Your kindness means more to me than you can imagine. I love every single story. I love every single dish. I feel I have now found peace for young Jill.

TAWANNA'S STORY

"And believe me, a good piece of chicken can make anybody believe in the existence of God."

—SHERMAN ALEXIE

TAWANNA "TSTYLES" "TEELATTRICE" SMITH—THE STORY OF GRANDMA MABEL'S FRIED CHICKEN, THE BEST FRIED CHICKEN ON EARTH!
Age 43, Hair Stylist

Out of the low-income housing in Toledo, Ohio, comes a story of love, neighbors, scratch cooking, and fried chicken.

Tawanna is a dear friend of mine and a beautiful soul. She is a creative hairdresser and an inspiring motivational speaker empowering women. Tawanna has the ability to lift people up with her words of encouragement and teaches how to look at life in the most positive way. Her career is just getting started; she has found her calling. Keep your light shining, my friend!

When Tawanna was about eleven, in the early 1990s, she lived with her grandmother, Mabel, who was one astounding and acclaimed cook in the neighborhood. Being raised by Mabel meant Tawanna and her two brothers were very lucky to be the primary recipients of this loving and astonishing cooking. The family lived in the housing projects in Toledo, meaning everyone lived very close together. However, due to the housing situation, if you cooked something, the aroma fanned all over the buildings, and when Mabel was making her famous fried chicken, the whole neighborhood knew and came out.

During World War II, there were Civil Defense Sirens — aka Air-Raid sirens, which were insanely loud — installed throughout the country; if there was ever danger coming, the air sirens would sound an alarm that could be heard from everywhere. Well, the same thing held true with Grandma Mabel's fried chicken — but no air siren was needed. Just the scent wafting through the neighborhood of luscious fried chicken in progress, in all its glory, brought everyone running with fingers crossed that they would score a piece.

When trying to decide which dish from her childhood to share, Tawanna, with passion in her voice, answered, "My grandmother's fried chicken was the best fried chicken ever, so yeah, I'll talk about her fried chicken." That decision didn't come lightly; there was stiff competition as she reminisced on the sweet potato pie and the greens — mouthwatering, but let's talk fried chicken!

Grandma Mabel made everything from scratch; there was no microwave growing up. Being used to their "ASAP" cooking through a microwave, Tawanna's friends used to laugh and comment that she had to wait for dinner. However, Tawanna proudly said she was happy to wait for her grandmother's home cooking. "When you had her food, it filled you up. You weren't hungry 20 minutes later. And you had leftovers for the next day." Try any of that with a microwave; there is something unique to be said for scratch cooking.

The preparation of the chicken is burned into Tawanna's mind from watching her grandma so many times. You can see the affection and fondness on her face as she describes it:

"She would take the chicken and soak it up really good in the vinegar. Then she would season her flour and put the chicken in a plastic bag, and shake it up. She would make sure that grease was really hot in the pan before putting the chicken in. No lid at first, then after it got kind of crispy, she would put the lid on it continuing to cook it inside the pan. As the last step, she would take the lid off, and that would allow it to really crisp up."

That chicken was, of course, cooked in a cast-iron pan. Cast-iron pans are extraordinary cooking vessels. They are relatively inexpensive compared to other cookware. Over time, the pan develops a coating known as "seasoning," which creates a beautiful non-stick surface. This allows you to cook anything with ease. They last forever, or almost forever, and are often passed down from one generation to another. By then, the natural non-stick would be well ingrained in the pan, making it perfect for cooking up your favorite family meals. And the best part of it all is that you are actually cooking with your past generations, for real. Lastly, cast-iron pans distribute heat evenly, which is excellent for cooking, let's say, fried chicken. But Mabel knew that.

"And when I tell you that her chicken was better than any restaurant I've ever eaten at ..." She mentioned with that all-knowing look you get when you are so certain of something. "It was the crispiest, juiciest, most flavorful chicken... Everybody in the neighborhood came to our house when she cooked chicken. She just passed it out, and everybody loved it."

After everyone got their piece, they would talk about it. "Your grandmother cooks the best chicken." "When is your grandmother cooking chicken again?" Even as kids grew into adults, they would come over. No matter where they lived, they made the trip. Mabel continued to cook and feed the neighborhood with her world's best fried chicken until she couldn't any longer.

What is not to love about this story? Well, perhaps one thing. The part Tawanna disliked the most was her job in the process—cleaning the chicken thighs. Mabel did all the cooking herself, minus the chicken thigh cleaning. Enter Tawanna.

"The process consisted of taking the chicken out of the package, putting it in the sink filled with cool water, letting it soak for at least fifteen minutes, and then removing as much fat from the chicken as possible," she explained with a distasteful expression." Then I had to do a final rinse on the chicken. I didn't like touching it. I didn't like removing the fat. It was something about the texture that I didn't like. To this day, some textures bother me. I had to clean at least three to four pounds; it would take me a minimum of at least forty-five minutes because I dreaded it so much."

Now Tawanna only buys boneless skinless chicken thighs; she is pretty much done with the cleaning job.

Mabel made sure to teach all of her grandchildren how to cook. And, aside from cleaning the chicken thighs, her philosophy was that kids should be kids, and she would handle the kitchen.

"My grandmother didn't really allow me in the kitchen to clean unless I was in trouble, so I never really had to wash dishes, only as a form of punishment. However, as I got a little older, like in my teens, she would explain what she was doing, teaching us as she was cooking. She enjoyed doing it so much. It was mainly around the holidays because other times I was outside enjoying my friends. Holidays were the times when she would be in the kitchen cooking all day and night, listening to music enjoying the holiday spirit."

Tawanna also fondly remembers learning how to make her famous turkey and dressing.

"One year during Christmas, we were in the kitchen around eleven at night, and she was teaching me how to make her famous turkey and dressing. We were listening to *Silent Night* by the Temptations. She was singing it and telling me what she was doing as she was doing it. It was always great watching her; she was so comfortable in the kitchen. It was her happy place." This sentiment makes me smile, as it's mine as well. I am honored to be in such wonderful company. Tawanna continues, "She cooked everything from scratch. I just remember the smile on her face, the aroma from the food as it was cooking, and the closeness I felt being in her presence. The thought of it brings a smile to my face and tears to my eyes because I wish I had more time and one last taste of her cooking."

Today Tawanna is an amazing cook, thanks in large part to her grandmother's lessons. She loves to cook and get lost in it, which is a tremendous place to be. Even though she doesn't fry much anymore, she does follow her grandmother's recipe, exactly as made, when she does. One day, she hopes to open a restaurant and call it "Mabel's Place." Of course, fried chicken will be on the menu. What a tribute that will be to this renowned and inspiring woman.

The only physical memories of Mabel that Tawanna has today are her bible and her silk headscarf, which she still wears proudly. I've seen it, and the scarf is just beautiful. It has a dark brown background with a white check overlay in the center in a rectangle shape, leaving a brown border around the outside and a beautiful splash of gold in the center. "I usually wear it to bed every night. It's been nine years." Such a beautiful honor to Mabel that I actually got goosebumps when she told me. She absolutely treasures the scarf and the bible.

Lucky for us, she also has the recipe for this legendary chicken which I will now share with you. Thank you, Mabel, so very much.

GRANDMA MABEL'S FAMOUS FRIED CHICKEN

This recipe is written as directly told to me by Tawanna through her memories of Mabel. I've added comments in places I felt would help clarify the recipe.

INGREDIENTS:

- 3-4 Lbs. Bone-in Chicken, Mabel used Legs and Thighs (and we now know how to clean the thighs)
- Water (see directions for measurement)
- White Vinegar (see directions for measurement)
- Your Favorite Seasonings to taste (see directions for particular spices and measurements)
- Flour (see directions for measurement)
- Vegetable or Canola Oil (see directions for measurement)

DIRECTIONS:

1. Take your chicken (bone-in, skin on, as much or little as you want) and soak it in equal parts water and vinegar for about 5 minutes (enough combined liquid to cover the chicken). Rinse well.
2. Pat the chicken dry with a paper towel. Season it with your favorite seasonings. Mabel used thyme, salt, pepper, and garlic powder (to your taste – about 1/2 – 1 teaspoon each).
3. Use a bowl, paper or plastic bag with flour in it and toss the chicken until it's evenly coated. Start with 1 cup flour and add more as needed.
4. Fill a skillet with cooking oil, enough to slightly cover the chicken, at medium-high heat until it's really hot, but not burning. Mable used cast iron which is best for this as the heat will maintain the oil temperature throughout

cooking, but use what you have. You can test the oil with a small amount of flour. When the flour starts frying, you know it's ready.

5. Place your chicken inside and put a lid on it. Cook for 8 minutes, then flip the chicken over. After you brown the other side, remove the lid. Cook the chicken while flipping both sides over again for another few minutes, until golden brown. For food safety, fried chicken is best when the internal temperature reaches 165. It is best to use a meat thermometer to test this.

6. Remove your beautiful chicken and place on a dish lined with paper towels to soak up any excess oil.

7. Enjoy!

IAN'S STORY

"If you really want to make a friend, go to someone's house and eat with him - the people who give you their food give you their heart."

—CESAR CHAVEZ

IAN SHORR — THE STORY OF LINGUINE AND HUMAN KINDNESS
Age 39, Writer/DJ/Panda Enthusiast

Ian is a very close friend who has received the nickname "Panda" simply because he resembles a panda in the most adorable way. To his friends, that is what he is often called. When he is not celebrating his spirit animal, he is a screenwriter, writing for television, among many other things. I love him dearly. I was so happy when he offered to share his childhood food memories. His story, as I suspected, didn't disappoint. Ian's latest of many projects was adapting the book *The Reincarnationist Papers* into the screenplay for Paramount's *INFINITE*, which was released on June 10, 2021. As luck would have it, the author of said book also has his childhood memory documented here in this book. Be sure not to miss Eric's story.

As Ian pondered what dish he wanted to share for this book, he imagined that most people would tell a story about a dish they had at home growing up. Or, as he called it, "domestic delights." While there were many dishes he could talk about like that, his story takes place thousands of miles away from home—in this case, home being Salt Lake City, Utah. However, this story stood out to him in particular; it's a perfect example of the power of food and the power of community.

This story took place when Ian was sixteen, traveling all across Europe in 1998. His parents had been looking for something to have him do for the summer since he was too old for camp. They found an enticing group called Interlock that did organized youth adventures. They signed him up to make a two-month-long, thousand-mile bike trip over the Alps and through cities starting in Venice, Italy and then ending in Paris, France. He set off on his bike with a group of eleven other kids and two adult guardians, a husband and wife. Being the adventurous type, he thought, "How long can a thousand miles be?"

It turned out to be an adventure that gave him memories to last a lifetime.

His story takes place in a small town in Italy, whose name, sadly, has been lost over the decades. On this particular night, the group pulled into town after riding sixty to seventy miles, exhausted, ready to eat, and get some sleep.

"The nightly routine was that a few of the kids would take the bike that had a trailer attached to it to the store and buy groceries for dinner. They would then make a big camp meal together." Ian reminisced.

But not on this night. The town they pulled into didn't have any campsites available, and they weren't allowed to set up tents in the park.

"By then, it was getting dark, and it was looking like we would have to ride another thirty miles to the next town."

They were all hungry and tired. Enter the power of community. By chance, they met the owner of the local YMCA, as Ian describes it. The owner's name was Giuseppe, and he and his wife said they could stay in the basketball gym overnight. The grateful group brought their belongings into the gym and set up their sleeping bags, relieved they had a roof over their head.

The kindness didn't end there. They next found out that the couple was going to make them an Italian feast for dinner. Ian then used the term "hunger is the best sauce," which carries the connotation that being hungry makes one less concerned about the taste of the food. However, they were about to have the most memorable meal of the entire trip, so much so for Ian that this is the one dish that brings him back to his childhood.

With a smile on his face, Ian continued, "We all sat down at a big table outside of the gym in a garden area to eat whatever was about to come our way. What was served is something I can still taste to this day. A big bowl of linguine came out to the table. There were maybe seven ingredients in it, but the flavor was so fresh and vivid. I actually remember saying to myself at age sixteen that this was the best meal I've ever had."

Since then, Ian has eaten at some amazing places — but this dish still ranks among his top five meals.

"We sat there serving ourselves heaping plates of linguine with diced tomatoes, sliced green olives, chunks of spicy Italian sausage, onions, peppers, fresh basil, and grated Pecorino Romano sprinkled all over the top. This was served with freshly baked sourdough bread that the wife had just made." The bread would steam as you broke it open.

With a small chuckle, Ian mentions, "The meals that we had been cooking were a lot of rice, a lot of starch, a lot of one-pot stuff that a group of sixteen-year-olds could cook together. Having something with that level of simple mastery to it was just another worldly experience for us." He goes on, "Giuseppe and his wife were impeccable hosts. Not only did they open their doors and let us sleep there, but they did not charge for the use of the gym, and they fed us for free as well."

It was human kindness at its finest. This encounter left a permanent mark in his head about how strangers can treat each other and make others feel welcome. Seeing the level of happiness around that table rewired something in his brain. When he thinks about how he got interested in cooking for people besides himself, that experience is probably behind it.

Ian is a fantastic cook. He is a true foodie and loves to replicate the wonderful meals he discovers in restaurants or during his travels. One of his most endearing traits is that he loves to cook for people. Feeding others is his gift and something he often does with true happiness and passion. I have been the recipient of his kindness on many occasions and had the tremendous pleasure of cooking for friends with him. And now, I am learning where at least part of the magic that is Ian comes from — that experience in a town in Italy with the forgotten name but indelible memories. If there were campsites available that night, all this would have never happened. It only happened because they ran into some adversity.

Hearing this story gave me such an "ah-ha" moment about him. I see this as a lesson in giving back. He never saw the couple again, but the kindness he still pays forward due to their actions is truly astonishing. He goes out of his way to help everyone. If you are hungry, he is there to cook for you. If you need help, he will be there. If it is a big problem, he will immediately summon his mass of friends to collectively and successfully rise to the challenge. Ian is one of the kindest, sincerest, and most giving human beings I have ever had the pleasure of knowing. Anyone that knows him will say the exact same thing.

While Ian did not get the recipe in Italy, he has been able to recreate it — through many trials. Everyone who has experienced this dish has loved it. In Ian's eyes, certain foods are so attached to a specific experience that some dishes, such as this one, really need the entire experience component to recreate it exactly the same. Even if he went to Italy to study cooking, he doesn't think he will ever exactly recreate the dish he had that night in the Italian YMCA given by an incredible, giving couple. Be good to each other. And, if you ever forget that, reread this story. In the meantime, try this amazing pasta.

LINGUINE WITH ITALIAN SAUSAGE

INGREDIENTS:
- 1 package linguine
- 1 pound spicy Italian sausage
- 1 large can diced tomatoes
- 5 cloves of garlic, diced
- 1 red onion, diced
- 1 cup of pitted green olives
- 2 tablespoons of capers
- 1/4 cup extra virgin olive oil
- sprinkle of dried oregano
- sprinkle of dried basil
- 1/2 cup finely shredded pecorino romano cheese

DIRECTIONS:
1. Boil the linguine according to package directions in salted water until al dente. While it's boiling/cooking, follow next steps.

2. Crumble the sausage in a large pan and cook with the olive oil over medium-high heat until browned and cooked through.
3. Once sausage has browned, mix in the diced onion, garlic, oregano, and basil.
4. After about 4–5 minutes, when the onion starts to get translucent, add in the large can of diced tomatoes with juice.
5. Next, add in olives.
6. Cover, reduce heat and simmer for 20 minutes.
7. Once sauce is complete, mix it into the pasta.
8. Sprinkle capers and romano across the top.
9. Serve with a fresh-baked baguette and a green salad.
10. Enjoy!

ERIC'S STORY

———

"Part of the secret of success is to eat what you like and let the food fight it out inside."

—MARK TWAIN

D. ERIC MAIKRANZ — THE STORY OF A WORKING SINGLE MOM, GRANDPARENTS AND THE WORLD OF CONVENIENCE FOODS

Age 55, Author

I met Eric through Ian. At the time, I had no idea that I would be writing a book and how invaluable his experience of being an author would be. Eric wrote the book *The Reincarnationist Papers*, which Ian Shorr's screenplay — as discussed in the previous chapter — was adapted from. Thank you so much for all of the support and advice you have given me.

I am truly grateful. Be on the lookout for Eric's next book, *The Cognomina Codex*.

Eric grew up in the poorest county in Southern Indiana in the 1970s. He was raised by his mom, Diana. They struggled some, but they never went hungry.

Eric's grandparents, Pauline and Dale, were both in the Army during World War II. They met while they were stationed in Texas, working in Quarter Mastery, which dealt in logistics and supplies. They made sure supplies such as food, clothing, and ammunition got on the ships or trains. Pauline was from Oklahoma; Dale was from Indiana. Eric is extremely proud of both of them and keeps a photo of them in their military uniforms to share with friends. After the war ended, they married and settled down in Dale's family home in Warrick County, Indiana — this is the area where Eric was born and grew up.

"I ended up spending a lot of time with my grandparents while my mom worked one or two jobs."

While considering which memories housed the one dish that brings him back to his childhood, Eric stated, "It actually brought back a lot for me that was mostly good, some not so good." This is such a great example of how some childhood food memories are not always positive and yet still have such a profound impact on us that we carry them over to our adult life. "Some not so good" isn't bad. We all learn early on, thanks to the amygdala, much of the foods we do and don't like.

"My mother and father divorced when I was young, so I was raised by a single mom. She was a real hero in my life for all of the things that she did. She always had at least two jobs and sometimes three to keep a roof over our heads and some food in the cupboard. Being from a very small town in rural Indiana, there was no support infrastructure for her other than my grandparents, which is why I stayed with them so often. It must have been so hard and so scary for her, but she was always very loving and supportive through it all."

Convenience food was a blessing to a working mom, and Eric ate a lot of prepackaged, processed foods growing up. Don't be fooled, though; they didn't just have the basic mac and cheese or instant pudding straight from the package. "It was always elevated up in some way," he recalled. Some of her elevated convenience food recipes still fondly stick in his mind. "She didn't just open a can and dinner was served. She took the time to take what was prepackaged and added her own special magic." I am thrilled to share the dishes that summon his childhood memories.

"Do you remember Dinty Moore beef Stew?" Eric asked me. "My mom would put that into a round glass casserole dish and then take a cylinder of premade biscuit dough and make a pattern on top with the biscuits to do an impromptu Shepherd's Pie kind of a thing." This would be a weekly thing in the rotation. "It was cheap and would last a few days for the two of us, and I just loved it!"

But the dish that brings him back to his childhood the most was Grandma Pauline's Banana Pudding, which like many dishes in Eric's life, is a convenience-based food. Her banana pudding was made from instant banana pudding mix. Grandma Pauline came from a time when convenience foods were rising in popularity.

Eric referenced my Tuna Noodle Casserole video on Yester-Kitchen, where I discussed how the 1950s was the beginning of the convenience food era. I discussed how some house-wives of the 1950s had been the working girls "Rosie the Riveters" of the 1940s, and not every woman left the workforce when World War II was over. So, when these women married and started families, there was not enough time to scratch cook dinner as women of decades prior did. Convenience food became very popular as a mom can start with pre-made meals then add her own spin on them with spices and flavors. This story resonated with Eric's own memories of his childhood, for which I am truly honored.

When making the banana pudding, Eric reminisces, "If I was a very good boy, meaning not breaking something for a few days, she would go the extra mile and make it from the packaged mix you had to cook on the stove. There was something extra special about it being cooked."

No matter which mix she used, it always included fresh bananas and Nabisco Nilla Wafers. No meringue, no whipped cream. Just simplicity at its finest. He absolutely loved it.

Meredith Bethune explains in her 2016 article, "The Sweet Success of Bananas Foster Has an Unsavory Past," that bananas were considered quite exotic here in America as recently as the late 1800s. Imports came from the West

Indies and landed in New Orleans. This belated introduction brought with it something very new and different, unlike any other fruit. They were being shipped in literally by the "boatload," and they had to be used quickly. So clever cooks started to come up with ways to use them. This need for spontaneous creativity is actually how Bananas Foster, a classic New Orleans dessert, was created — but that is a story for another day.

Home cooks across the country attempted to make their own banana pudding. However, this was usually just banana-flavored vanilla pudding and not the actual banana pudding, with the bananas added that we know today. Yet, as development and creativity grew, additions started being added to the pudding, such as sponge cake and ladyfingers.

In 1900, a company by the name of National Biscuit Company, or Nabisco,came out with Nilla Wafers. They started gaining fans almost immediately. In Aaron Hutcherson's 2020 article, "Like, it's Complicated History, Banana Pudding has Many Layers," he tells the 1921 story of how Mrs. Laura Kerley submitted her recipe for Banana Pudding, including the wafers, to a newspaper in Bloomington, Illinois, called the *Pentagraph*. This very recipe was what catapulted Banana Pudding with Nilla Wafers to stardom. Everyone started making it, sharing it, loving it. Due to its immense popularity, in 1940, Nabisco started printing the recipe right on the box, and they do so to this day. The rest, as they say, is history.

Years later, when Eric was grown and married, he brought his wife back to his hometown of Elberfeld. The total population was about one thousand, with only two bars to its name.

One was the American Legion Hall. The American Legion in Warrick County had a cookbook created by the locals who submitted their recipes. Of course, Eric bought one.

When he got home and started looking through the cookbook, he realized that he wasn't alone in his love of all things convenience food. The recipes included things you could make with Miracle Whip, Hamburger Helper, boxed macaroni and cheese, and all other sorts of delightful, pre-packaged foods. It reminded him that everything he ate as a kid came out of a jar, package, or box. This ongoing familiarity is probably why even as a foodie today, he still enjoys guilty pleasures such as his beloved can of Dinty Moore Beef Stew. Everything comes back to childhood.

"I love convenience foods, and in a way, they are like a comfort food for me. I certainly eat better now than I did as a kid, but I love my packaged snacks and prepared foods." In a follow-up email for this story, Eric informed me that he succumbed to a guilty pleasure the night before by making Hamburger Helper. I fully support his dinner decision.

Here is Eric's childhood memory of his Grandma's Banana Pudding. Of course, this is very convenience food-based. If you are short on time, this recipe is for you! If you have been good, make the cooked pudding version. Both are equally delicious!

GRANDMA PAULINE'S BANANA PUDDING

INGREDIENTS:

- 1 Box instant banana flavored pudding (or the cooking required variety, if you have been good)
- 1–2 Bananas (depending on the size of your serving dish)
- 1 Box "Nilla' Wafers (You may not need the entire box, but they are wonderful for snacking)

DIRECTIONS:

1. Prepare the box of instant banana pudding according to the package directions.
2. Once you have pudding, stir in slices of fresh bananas.
3. Line a serving bowl with Nilla Wafers around the side, preferably a clear bowl so you can see the wafers.
4. Pour pudding and banana mix in the center and top with more Vanilla Wafers.
5. Enjoy!

RICK'S STORY

———

"No one who cooks, cooks alone. Even at her most solitary, a cook in the kitchen is surrounded by generations of cooks past."
—LAURIE COLWIN

RICK SCOT–THE STORY OF JEWISH PENICILLIN AND ONE VERY SPECIAL GRANDMA
Age 52, Brother

Rick is my brother from another mother. I don't even like to say that since he has been a real brother to me, and I love him very much. For all intents and purposes, he is my brother. My kids call him "Uncle Rick." We go way back, and the relationship is beyond special.

We met when we were in our early twenties, two kids just starting out in the working world. I was a manager at The

Broadway in Century City, CA. If this doesn't ring a bell, this department store was bought out by Macy's in 1995. I needed an additional salesperson, and one day I received a call from Human Resources asking me to come down and interview someone. Little did I know this person would become a massive part of my life. I hired him and the rest, as they say, is history.

I have heard many wonderful stories about his family over the years, but it was a welcome surprise to hear about some of his family members I have not had the honor to meet. Rick has a very special childhood memory about food, which is delicious and honors someone special that is no longer with us.

Rick's memory is of his Grandma Audrey's Chicken and Matzoh Ball Soup, otherwise known as Jewish Penicillin. When I originally asked Rick via email to contribute to this book, this magic elixir called chicken soup was the first thing that came to his mind. It was his childhood. It was his memories. It was pure comfort. Besides being delicious, this original homemade soup is known to have properties to cure the common cold, and it almost always works. The exact properties might be love, comfort, and the fact that it is unlikely to upset the stomach. Grandma Audrey made this every Passover, the major Jewish celebration that commemorates the Israelites' liberation from Egyptian slavery. This is a big family and friend's dinner, which usually includes the aforementioned Chicken Soup. Matzoh, an unleavened bread similar to a large cracker, is used for this holiday exclusively since bread is not allowed.

Her extraordinary soup was only made for special occasions, and she especially loved to make it for her grandchildren. "I don't have a first memory of this soup because it has always been in my life," Rick starts, "it's a very personal memory for me. But I've had this as long as I can remember. Even when we went somewhere else for Passover, I would go to her house just to have a bowl of her soup after." He describes it as being like a hug from grandma.

This soup is such an integral part of his childhood. Although she made so many different dishes while he was growing up, this is the only one he remembers.

When he was twenty-three, he was living in Los Angeles. His grandparents had moved to Florida by this time, but they were visiting Palm Springs for this particular Passover. He drove from LA to Palm Springs. "The weather was one hundred million degrees," Rick remarked, a usual temperature for that town. However, he really wanted a bowl of her soup regardless of the heat outside, so he asked her to make it, and she happily obliged her grandson. Matzoh ball soup is served hot and usually reserved for weather less than 100 million degrees, but this was that important to him. Ultimately, it was the last time he was able to enjoy the soup with her before she passed away. Rick describes this as "a very special time where I got to watch her make the soup and then enjoy our time together over a bowl." She had Parkinson's and was not able to cook like she used to so this day was even more special since she took the extra efforts in making this dish for him. Matzoh ball soup takes time to make; sometimes taking all day to simmer the chicken to achieve the ultimate result of a rich broth. He cherishes that time with her to this day.

"The Matzoh balls were light and fluffy because she beat the egg whites separate." This procedure is a very non-traditional way of making matzoh balls, as it is customary to use the whole egg. "I worked to replicate the memories through her recipe." The broth was made from scratch; it was delicious and rich. His grandma's recipe for this dish is different from the standard one — and lucky for us, he is willing to share.

Rick, fondly remembering this last visit, continued, "We spent a great deal of time talking about Passover's past. We discussed family gatherings. I remember making fun of my grandfather and his constant need to have a thirty-two-ounce iced tea in his hand. Funny thing is that I do the same thing." This tradition is yet another wonderful example of what we bring into adulthood from our childhood experiences.

"My grandma talked a bit about growing up in a Jewish home where the women cooked, and she was always asked to help in the kitchen. She didn't love it, and although she would make Passover dinner every year, cooking was not something she enjoyed doing, and didn't think she was very good at it." Rick relayed with a perplexed face. Though, in reality, it seems like she actually was very good, as evidenced by Rick's childhood memory. "I wish she knew how good of a cook she was. I hope deep down she did."

Rick continues his story, "We talked about my father, and I learned a little about his history as a child. How he spent the first six years of his life in Japan with his family right after the end of World War II. My grandfather was in the Army Air Guard." A family member once told me that the Army Air Guard was the precursor to the Air Force — also known as the Army Air Corps, were units that flew back before the Air Force was created in 1947 and may have been referred to as the Army Air Guard.

"She shared so much that visit, we even talked about Florida, where they were living." Rick reminisces, "They missed living in Palm Springs and didn't necessarily enjoy Florida as much. They missed having their friends close by, although they enjoyed visiting with them during this visit."

Rick was only twenty-three at the time, but even at fifty-two, he remembers it like it was yesterday. Merging great food and warm memories allows you to travel back every time.

This dish, although special, was something he never made himself until after she passed. It was Grandma Audrey's calling to make it, which Rick did not complain one bit about. Yet after she passed, he kept her tradition alive by making her soup. Truly, a beautiful tribute.

Rick doesn't make it often since the soup is a lot of work. Yet, oh-so-worth the effort when it is made. This is why it's a common dish usually reserved for holidays and special occasions. Sure, you can find it in a Jewish deli, hopefully made properly with the rich broth and deep chicken flavor, but why not try your luck at creating a memory with it by making it at home on a special day.

There are as many recipes for Chicken Soup with Matzoh Balls as there are families that make it. Grandma Audrey's recipe is time-consuming yet worth every minute. Please enjoy it with Rick's compliments.

GRANDMA AUDREY'S CHICKEN SOUP AND MATZOH BALLS

Audrey's matzoh balls are far more flavorful when cooked in a delicious chicken soup (the recipe of which has also been provided below). However, in a pinch, you can cook them in boiling water and add them to already prepared chicken soup.

MATZOH BALLS INGREDIENTS:
- 1 cup of Matzo Meal
- 4 large eggs, separated
- 1 teaspoon kosher salt
- 4 tablespoons flavorless oil (canola, vegetable, grape seed) or schmaltz (chicken fat)
- 2 teaspoons baking powder

DIRECTIONS:
1. Separate the eggs, placing the yolks into a bowl with oil or schmaltz, mix to break up the eggs.
2. In a separate bowl, combine the matzo meal, salt, and baking powder.
3. Next, whip the egg whites with an electric mixer until soft peaks form.
4. Combine the egg yolk and oil mixture with the dry ingredients, mix until combined. (do not over mix)
5. Fold in the egg whites to combine all ingredients. Be gentle at this stage.
6. Let the batter rest in the refrigerator for at least 2 hours.
7. This is a good time to start making the chicken soup (below) if you choose to use that.
8. After the time has passed, have your chicken soup strained and boiling or bring a large pot of water to a rolling boil

that will hold about 24 matzoh balls (depending on the size of the ball).

9. Take a teaspoon of the batter (a tablespoon if you want larger matzo balls) and roll it into a ball with wet hands. This will prevent sticking.
10. Carefully, drop matzoh balls into the prepared soup (recipe below) or boiling water.
11. Do not overcrowd the pot, as they will rise to the top and expand when cooked. You can cook the matzoh balls in batches if your pot isn't large enough. Simply remove and set aside the balls as they cook. Everything will go back into the pot once they are all cooked.
12. Once they've all risen to the top, turn the water down to a simmer and cook for 40 minutes.

CHICKEN SOUP INGREDIENTS:

Here's an easy recipe to make while the matzo ball mixture is resting. (This one is Rick's recipe)

- 2 tablespoons butter
- 1 yellow onion
- 3 cloves of garlic
- 3 stalks of celery
- 1 whole leek
- 1 carrot
- 1 teaspoon ginger (fresh)
- 4 cups chicken stock
- 3 boneless, skinless chicken breasts, or one rotisserie chicken shredded

DIRECTIONS:

1. Place the butter into the bottom of a large pot to melt over medium heat.

2. To that pot over medium heat, sauté the onions, celery, carrots, and leek together until soft.

3. Then, add the garlic and ginger to the pot and soften; this will take just a few minutes.

4. Next, add the stock and let simmer (If you're using chicken breast, add them at this point and let it simmer in the pot for at least one hour. You can then shred the chicken breasts. If using an already cooked rotisserie chicken, add the chicken 10 minutes before serving to heat the chicken through.)

5. Strain out the chicken and vegetables and set them aside, reserve the stock in the pot.

6. This is the time to add the raw matzoh balls to the soup.

7. Once the matzoh balls are done, add the chicken and vegetables back into the soup with the matzoh balls and serve everyone some soup, chicken, vegetables, and one or two matzoh balls.

8. Enjoy!

JILL'S STORY

"A good restaurant is like a vacation; it transports you, and it becomes a lot more than just about the food."

—PHILIP ROSENTHAL

JILL HECKER—THE STORY OF RESTAURANTS AND MY DADDY, THE FOODIE

Age 55, Culinary Storyteller/Mom/Retro Aficionado/Devoted Cook/Founder of YesterKitchen

I have my daddy, Shelly, to thank for introducing me to so many things that make me who I am. I also have him to thank for the dishes that bring me back to my childhood. There are two main dishes that I love equally, and we will explore one of them here. It may be a surprise to learn that my dishes were not home-cooked, although I've enjoyed many wonderful ones. Rather, they are from two different restaurants that had an impact on me, helping to shape my lifelong fascination for food, taking me back every time.

Restaurants of the past have stories to tell. They share what food and life were like during their time. Just reading a menu from one of these places of history is like peeking into a time capsule. The menu design, the food, the prices, the descriptions of the dishes. They are beautiful signs of the times, a wonderful edible history lesson. And my daddy introduced me to this world, back when these wonderful eating establishments still existed.

When I have the opportunity to dine at a restaurant that has been around for many decades, I am in heaven. I can feel the history of a place when I walk through the front doors. Having the opportunity to dine at many remarkable restaurants as a child gave me an appreciation for more than just the food. I appreciated the entire dining experience. It brought so much joy to read menus, pick my favorite dish, experience exceptional service, and taste such exquisite food. I fell in love with restaurants — from diners to fine dining and everything in between.

My dad took me to some of the best restaurants Los Angeles had to offer. This was the 1970s, and I didn't realize that it wasn't common for a ten-year-old to be immersed in so much food culture. Today, my gratitude and appreciation for that time are immeasurable.

There is no way to count the number of restaurants I was lucky enough to experience. However, upon digging deep into my memories, there are two exceptionally unique restaurants — along with their special dishes — that I hold dear. One is long gone, one happily remains. They exemplify my love of the dining experience. Both contributed to my passion for sharing dishes of the past so that they don't get lost in history. We will revisit Lawry's the Prime Rib, along with their famed recipe, in the bonus chapter at the end of this book. For now, it is my honor to share my memory of an Old West-themed amusement park that started with a humble berry stand.

According to Janie Ellis's 2020 article "The History of Knott's Berry Farm," Knott's Berry Farm started with the boysenberry created by Walter Knott in the early 1920s. I shared the history of Knott's Berry Farm and how to make their world-famous boysenberry pie on my channel — in a video aptly titled "Boysenberry Pie" — using a recipe right from my Knott's Berry Farm cookbook.

I loved Knott's and wanted to spend most of my time in Ghost Town, which hearkened back to a time of the old west, including saloons, cowboys, gunfights, a Calico Railway train, an old cemetery with very funny headstones, and stagecoaches. So much old west. So much history. I loved it. Today, much of what I remember about Ghost Town has been removed or changed, yet the town lives on as it was in my memory.

After a day at the park, it was dinner time. We always went to the same place: "The Steak House," located in Ghost Town. That was its name, simple and perfect. The restaurant was designed to be a work of art, celebrating California's early days. It was a huge beautiful building made of adobe bricks that were originally made right in the park. The Steak House opened in 1946. It had three huge dining rooms with very high ceilings. There was the Cowboy Room in honor of, well, the cowboys of the old west with massive portraits of famous cowboys on the walls. The next dining room was the more formal Walter Knott room dedicated to the park's namesake. They were stunning, but there was one that was extra special.

My favorite dining room was known as the Indian Room. I know it is respectful to now use the term "Native American," and I do, but this was the name back then. It was designed to respect and honor our earliest Americans and celebrate their culture. The décor was larger than life, and I always asked if we could sit in there. The problem was that everyone else did, too. It was a masterpiece. We didn't always get to sit in there. That goes to show how many times I've been fortunate enough to go and why I know about the other rooms.

This room was magnificent and was the only room that did not change names and décor the entire time the Steak House was around. This room was the largest of all. Gourds and dried chili peppers hung from the ceiling. The walls were covered with beautiful portraits of famous Native Americans such as Sitting Bull, Geronimo, and Crazy Horse. The tables we sat at were big and looked as if they were cut from a large piece of wood. They had small lamps on them, and the tables and chairs had Native American picture symbols— referred to as "pictography" — painted on them. The chairs were fashioned after tom-toms, or drums, with a simple back to lean against. Bare trees were set around the room. A rare unfinished rug was on display as well as blankets, a papoose, and other magnificent artifacts to celebrate the culture.

This restaurant spoke to my love of food and history. I felt at home. I didn't fully realize this until years later when I looked back with curiosity, wondering why I was so drawn to this restaurant. Childhood experiences once again contribute to who you become as an adult.

Steak was a popular option on the menu, but there was only one dish that I ordered. On the menu, it was called "Pioneer Beef Stew." In my 1976 cookbook, which I got at the park that year, it was called "Steak House Stew." Either way, it was delicious. As the menu describes it, it is a "rich beef stew filled with garden-fresh vegetables cooked as the Miners liked it in the days of '49." And, of course, that would be 1849. It was impeccable. It really was just a traditional beef stew filled with carrots, potatoes, onions, and tomatoes, all swimming in a delicious beef gravy. I think the restaurant's décor made it taste better. I still make it to this day, right from my cookbook.

The heavenly stew was served with salad, their famous hot rolls — well, they were called rolls on the menu but, in reality, were actually biscuits — and boysenberry jam. I don't remember much of the salad, but oh, the rolls. They were the same ones you would get at Mrs. Knott's Chicken Dinner Restaurant, which is still open and also one of my favorites. The rolls were small, buttery, and classic, and they brought you as many as you wanted.

Along with the rolls, the table would receive a soup cup size of real Knott's Berry Farm boysenberry preserves which are the best you can get. You just stuck your knife in, spread away, and you had one happy belly. That was the 1970s. By the 1980s, the cups of jam were replaced with the white plastic containers of jam where you peel off the top. This is just the way things are now, but I loved the family-style cup of preserves. I am so grateful that I got to experience that. Sadly, the Steak House closed its doors in the mid-1990s to make room for a roller coaster.

I loved this dish so much that I decided to create my own version of Pioneer Stew at home. Twelve-year-old me took beef jerky and heated it up in a pan, then added beef broth with — I think — garlic and pepper. Then right before serving, I sprinkled potato chips right on top; they would get soggy and mimic the potatoes in the stew. I made this all the time for myself. Was it beef stew? No. Was it delicious? To me, yes. Was it meaningful? Absolutely!

This was the beginning of my love affair with food, and I haven't stopped since. I would go to wonderful restaurants and, like my daddy, go home and try my best to replicate what I ate. From there, my love of food and cooking just grew to where I am today. And right around then, I started reading cookbooks, which only added to my fascination with all things culinary.

My daddy passed away in 2010. I still miss him every day. I feel as if I am carrying on his passion and his appreciation for food. As difficult as my experiences at school were, I had him, and I am so grateful. My daddy was my superhero. He influenced so many of my loves and interests. He also played football for UCLA — I had to add that in!

Allow me to transport you back to dinner time at Knott's Berry Farm. You don't need to sit in a beautifully decorated dining room to love this. It's uncomplicated and feeds your soul. It just may inspire you to recreate the meals you love from restaurants too.

KNOTT'S BERRY FARM'S PIONEER BEEF STEW

INGREDIENTS:
- ¼ cup oil
- 2 medium onions
- 3 garlic cloves, minced
- 4 lbs. beef, cut for stew meat (round or chuck work best)
- 1 28 oz can tomatoes with liquid
- 1 cup dry red wine (such as cabernet and pinot noir)
- 2 tablespoons Worcestershire
- 1 bay leaf
- 1 teaspoon basil
- 1 tablespoon parsley, chopped
- 2 potatoes, diced
- 3 lbs. carrots, Diced
- 3 stalks celery, diced
- 1 16 oz can corn, drained
- 1 15 oz can lima beans, drained
- Salt and pepper to taste

DIRECTIONS:
1. In a large dutch oven, heat oil and sauté onions and garlic until soft over medium heat.
2. Add meat and brown on all sides.

3. Then, add tomatoes, wine, Worcestershire, bay leaf, parsley, salt, and pepper. Give it a mix to blend flavors.
4. Simmer partially covered for 1 hour over medium heat.
5. While that pot is simmering, using a separate burner, combine potatoes, carrots, and celery in a medium saucepan with 1 cup water and cook until they are a little tender but still firm.
6. After meat has simmered for an hour, add the vegetables and remaining ingredients.
7. Continue cooking until meat is tender, about 15–20 minutes.
8. Enjoy!

ROD'S STORY

"The discovery of a new dish does more for the happiness of the human race than the discovery of a star."

—JEAN ANTHELME BRILLAT-SAVARIN

ROD HECKER–THE STORY OF THE PICKY EATER AND MOM'S AMAZING CHEESECAKE

Age 55, Grandpa/Wanderer

I am especially excited to share this story. I had the pleasure of learning something new about the man I'm married to; Rod is the love of my life, my partner in crime, and my husband. We've been together since 2002 and married since 2007. We have six, yes, count 'em, six kids, and two grandkids at the time of writing this.

He's supportive of my dream to build my YouTube, and Rod has been a guest on YesterKitchen three times. If you would like to see him, check out my episodes for Swiss Mustard Steak, The History of Nachos, and the Smoked Old Fashioned, where he takes charge and teaches how to make the cocktail. He is my greatest cheerleader, and I am very grateful.

While not playing pickleball, camping, or riding his dirt bike, Rod spends his time thoroughly enjoying his newfound retirement and being the social butterfly that he is.

Rod's childhood food memory takes place in the 1970s. He was around five or six at the time. Rod and his family lived in Newbury Park, CA, a suburb in Southern California, only about fifteen miles away from the first house he and I lived in together. Newbury Park is a beautiful suburban town about an hour outside of Los Angeles, two hours if you count Los Angeles traffic.

In my humblest opinion, the 1970s were such a wonderful time for food. Now that I think of it, these were the dishes I grew up with, so they have a very special place in my heart. For family dinners, casseroles were an easy dinner solution for the busy mom. Cream of mushroom soup and onion soup mix were extremely popular, and there was a myriad of recipes using these ingredients. Mixing either of these two with meat, vegetables, and sometimes pasta and dinner was served. These fabulous dishes were creamy, budget-friendly, filling, and packed with pure comfort — if you happen to enjoy mixed ingredients, that is.

However, Rod was a very picky eater as a child. For instance, he would only eat a hamburger with just the bun. No condiments, no lettuce, no tomato. Definitely no onions; he can't stand them, even to this day — much to my dismay. "There were very few foods I would eat." He reminisced. He couldn't stand when any food on his plate touched or mixed with another food. Everything had to be kept separate. Everything. "I wouldn't eat casseroles of any kind because the food was all "mushed" together. All food had to be in its place and stay there."

So, with that, his mom, Cindy — in her distinctly clever manner — made him a deal. He wasn't forced to eat things most of the time, but he did have to take a bite and try — just one single bite. Lucky for me, I was able to ask my mother-in-law about my husband's picky eating before she passed in December 2021. She told me some wonderful stories. Sorry, not sorry, honey.

"The first time I knew Rod was a picky eater, he was still in his highchair. His grandma Frankie was there and told me it was time to let him try scrambled eggs. I hadn't thought about that, so I made some and put them on his highchair tray. He stuck his little finger in it and gagged. I couldn't believe it."

"He didn't even taste them, he just touched them and gagged," said Cindy. "That was the start of his pickiness." She was still in disbelief over the eggs at the time of this interview. Has Rod changed his mind about scrambled eggs? His response was, "I'll eat them, but they are not high on my list." Thankfully, he doesn't gag anymore.

Cindy continued, "Everything was an ordeal until he got girlfriends that cooked. Then all of a sudden, he loved the vegetables that he wouldn't touch at home." She laughed, shaking her head. Girls, go figure.

Cindy always felt sorry for him when they would go to someone's house for dinner. "He would take his plate through the entire buffet and come out with black olives, a big pile of shredded cheese, chips, and if they had plain beef, he would have that." Before they went to the house, Rod would ask his mom what they were having, so she would have to talk to the hostess to find out the menu. According to Rod, "it didn't change anything about the evening, but at least I knew what I was in for. Or how hungry I would be after." It was a challenge.

His childhood food memory has everything to do with his picky eating. One day his mom made a new dessert — cherry cheesecake — for the family. Cindy got the recipe from her Aunt Donna Lee in Oklahoma. Rod remembers this day, "Prior to this, my only dessert experiences were ice cream, basic cakes, and cookies." Rod could usually smell things to tell if he would like something or not. I guess that goes back to his scrambled egg experience as a baby. He actually remembers sniffing the cheesecake and thinking, "It doesn't smell too bad; it might be okay." The smell of sweet cherries gave him the feeling that this was worth a try — even though, as with any cheesecake, there are no separate ingredients. The crust is connected to the filling, which is connected to the cherries.

He took a bite and was pleasantly surprised. This was delicious. Really delicious. "Growing up, most of my meals were plain, consisting of some kind of meat and vegetables. And those were either corn or peas. This dessert had color — bright red cherries. This was the first thing that was all mixed together and was colorful and different. I didn't even know that I liked cherries before this dish came along."

Game changer! Since it was a dessert, and immediately his favorite dessert, from then on, he always asked his mom to make it. Alas, the five-year-old had to learn that cheesecake couldn't be considered dinner.

Cherry cheesecake was his birthday "cake" request for many years. "Every year, I asked Mom to make this for my birthday. And that went on until I went away to college."

After interviewing Rod, I immediately called my mother-in-law to get the recipe. I had to see what dish made such an impact on him. I wanted to see if this dish would still bring him smiles and memories. Cindy did not disappoint. This is what I loved about her: She gave me the recipe, but I received it in the mail instead of email, written out. The recipe was so easy; it's a no-bake cheesecake that you make in a 9x13 inch pan instead of a springform pan in which cheesecakes are usually made — it literally can't get any easier.

One night, we happened to have several friends over, and I surprised him with this dessert. As soon as I took it out of the fridge, he immediately got a big smile. However, the proof is in the pudding, as they say. I served him a big piece first and waited. It didn't take long for him to say, "That's it!"

And just like that, he was five again—and my day was made. I had created smiles and memories alike from one no-bake cheesecake. Mission accomplished.

This cheesecake is so special that I was inspired to film an episode about the history of cheesecake, making this very recipe during it and sharing a picture of my beautiful mother-in-law, giving credit where it was due. If you are interested in seeing any of the videos I've mentioned in this story, check out The History of Cheesecake and the Roman Empire at YesterKitchen on YouTube.

I am happy to report that Rod is no longer the picky eater he used to be — well, mostly, that is — which is a good thing for both of us. He is definitely not the foodie that I am, but he loves my cooking. Phew! We have a deal, I cook, and he cleans up. I truly think I got the better end of the deal, yet so does he. Rod is not a fan of cooking, and I hate doing dishes, so our relationship works out perfectly.

It's surprising that pretty much everything I make has ingredients that are mixed up. I love to cook Asian, Mexican, Italian, and — given my love of retro — casseroles. "I love most of what Jill cooks." He's being honest, I do have a few mishaps, but I don't think I would do well making some meat with separate vegetables every night. Variety is the spice of life, and I am grateful that now he thinks so too.

Without further ado, here is Cindy's cheesecake. Maybe it will cure the picky eater in your life.

CINDY'S CHERRY CHEESECAKE

INGREDIENTS:
- ¾ cups butter (1 ½ sticks), melted
- 2 tablespoons Sugar
- 3 cups graham cracker crumbs
- 2 8 oz packages of cream cheese
- 1 lb. (2 cups) powdered sugar
- 2 teaspoons almond extract
- 12 oz container frozen whipped topping, thawed
- 1–2 cans cherry pie filling

DIRECTIONS:
1. Using a hand mixer, combine the butter and sugar in a medium bowl.
2. Next, add in graham cracker crumbs and mix well until combined.
3. Press the mixture into a 9x13 baking dish.
4. Bake at 350F for 8–12 minutes. Watch it bake; you want it to be light brown. Remove from the oven and let it cool.
5. In a medium bowl with a hand mixer, thoroughly mix the cream cheese, powdered sugar, and almond flavoring.
6. Taste, and if more almond flavor is desired, add another teaspoon or two until you get the flavor you want.
7. Then, fold in whipped topping.
8. Spread the cream cheese mixture over the graham cracker crust.
9. Top with 1–2 cans cherry pie filling, depending on how much you want. Chill at least two hours before serving.
10. Enjoy!

CINDY'S STORY

"You don't need a silver fork to eat good food."

—PAUL PRUDHOMME

CINDY WALKER—THE STORY OF SNOW ICE CREAM AND THE POWER OF IMAGINATION DURING WORLD WAR II

Age 79 at passing, Wife/Mom/Grandma/Great Grandma/ Child to God

This is a very special story to write. Cindy was my wonderful, loving mother-in-law. She always looked for the best in everyone and had such a positive outlook on life. The family dynamic was essential to Cindy, and she was one of those people that you would be lucky to have as part of your family. She was kind, sincere, caring, and always made whoever she was talking to feel special. I am honored to share her story about life on the farm during World War II. Sadly, Cindy passed away in December 2021, while this book was still in development. I miss her so much; she was such a loving inspiration to me and everyone that knew her. I wish I could hear her say, "Well Darlin'…" in her Oklahoma accent one more time.

Cindy's story starts in 1944 in Yale, Oklahoma, spending time on her grandmother Daisy Mae's farm when she was just two years old. "I spent time on the farm since I could almost walk," she remembers. These memories are from when she was a young child, but her visits to the farm span until she graduated from the University of Oklahoma. The farm is still there to this day, and family members still own it, although she hasn't been back since she left college.

World War II was in progress and her family, including her extended family, visited the farm as much as possible. As it was WWII, all the able men were off at war. Since they were a large and close family, the women and children wanted to spend as much time together as possible. Thus, the farm became their sanctuary — which is perhaps the reason why family meant so much to her.

During the war, you had to invent your own fun, and when you had several small children on the farm, you got resourceful. "We were kind of desperate. We didn't have any games to play." Cindy recalled. That is where brilliant imagination stepped in. Everything was a game. Cindy's Uncle Paige would call the kids to the barn and tell them to line up. He would then take the cow's utter and squirt milk into their mouths. The game was to see if the milk made it in, and the kids loved it.

Wartime cooking was a challenge. Food rationing was in effect, and families had to get creative to make meals when dealing with the reduction or lack of ingredients. "We knew there were certain things we couldn't eat, so we could save it for our soldiers. One of them was gum — as rubber was rationed — which stands out in my memory."

The article "Rationing" from the National World War II Museum tells us that sugar was one of the first things to be rationed. We were importing most of our sugar, and at the time, many of the ships that were used to import goods were turned into warships. In addition, it wasn't the safest thing to be a ship out in the ocean during wartime. So much of what we did have went to the soldiers fighting overseas and here at home. Towards the end of the war, most ingredients were rationed with the exception of milk, eggs, and vegetables, as we had plenty of supply here in the United States.

When Cindy's family was cooking and ran out of something, they didn't go to the store; they instead substituted another ingredient.

"It's just something you did. I can remember Mama saying, 'We'll substitute such and such.' It was kind of a way of life during wartime. Many of the women didn't have cars or knew how to drive. I remember walking to the stores." Cindy shared.

Another thing that was rationed was nylons. This was back when nylons had a seam going up the back of the leg. Cindy related a very funny story. It is so interesting to look at how life was and have that reaction because it is so far from what we experience today. According to Cindy, "The older girls would take eyebrow pencils and draw a line up the back of their legs, so it looked like they were wearing nylons. It was a different world back then, but it was all we knew."

The farm offered a sense of community for the adults while keeping the kids entertained.

Cindy's great-grandfather started the farm during the Oklahoma Land Rush in 1889. During this time, her great-grandfather got sick for a day, and her great-grandma Lucinda—who she is named after—took over and got on the horse to help stake out the land. That's just how it was out on the farm; no sick days, only work. Someone had to keep things going.

"The farm had cows, bulls, chickens, lambs, and pigs. And they grew alfalfa. All kinds of things. I remember grandma would be out there sometimes wringing a chicken's neck." Just another day on the farm. "My uncle would take us out (there was a medical condition that prevented him from going to war) and let us ride the pigs. He would hold our hands, and we would ride the pigs."

There was no indoor plumbing at the farmhouse. "We didn't have electricity and used outhouses," she recalls. "There was always a slop bucket under the bed in case any of the kids had to go in the middle of the night. In the morning, the bucket needed to be emptied, and the kids had to take turns taking out the bucket." Cindy absolutely hated the task, and I can't blame her.

Cindy went on to say, "The bathtub was a big old metal tub. They would heat the water and fill it. They didn't have stoves; they would have to use wood." Everyone took turns in the same bathtub water; you couldn't waste it. "We would start, I think, with the youngest, and then we would go up to the oldest in order of who could take a bath when. That was always kind of interesting."

Going to the farm was a race and Cindy always asked her mom, Frankie, to drive faster and faster. There was a good reason for this. Whoever got there first got dibs on who got to sleep next to grandma. At night, grandma would lay down and stretch out her arms, and the grandkids would sleep next to her. "If there were more kids there than would fit, they had to sleep with grandpa, and he had wool blankets that were very itchy, so no one wanted that." Grandma could fit six kids with her, all in her arms and all in order of who arrived. Everyone wanted the inside spot. Can you picture that? "I don't know how she slept with all those kids in her arms all night long."

There was more fun invented on the farm, which really goes to Daisy Mae's imagination. Even chores became a game. One of the big treats came when you turned four years old. You got to wash and dry the dishes. The kids really got excited. Another game was when grandma invited "Mrs. Lukenbacker" over. For this special visit, the girls would put on their dresses, get their dolls, and come downstairs. Around the kitchen table were chairs for everyone, including an empty chair. Mrs. Lukenbacker did not exist, but grandma would ask her the kids questions and tell the kids her answers. It was pure, honest entertainment. "We never questioned why we couldn't see her."

Cindy's grandma could invent anything to entertain kids. Imagination is just unreal, and Daisy Mae's imagination kept bored little kids happily occupied during the war on the farm, not even realizing that so many things were scarce.

"We had the most wonderful times on the farm and never spent a penny on any games or anything like that."

Amid the chaos of war, Cindy's favorite childhood food memory emerges. Snow ice cream. Of course, this was a winter-only treat. When it snowed, it was magical.

There were two rules when it came to snow ice cream. The first rule is that you can't eat the first snow of the year because there could be impurities in the air or ground. So, it had to be the second snow of the year. The second rule is probably one we all know, do not eat yellow snow. For the uninitiated, yellow snow meant someone relieved themselves on the snow. Or in Cindy's case on the farm, one of the animals could have done that as well.

"When Mama would send us out with the big plastic bowl to gather the second snow of the year, we had to be sure it was really white and pure. That's how it started out, and it was so exciting. When the second snow happened, we got so excited because we knew we'd be playing cards and eating snow ice cream. It was a big excitement."

Making snow ice cream was a common thing to do in the winter for the area.

"During winter visits, the kids couldn't wait for the second snow. Ice cream was never purchased from the store."

Snow ice cream was more than just the ice cream. It was a special experience of the process from the time they gathered the snow to when they actually made the ice cream. Of course, the best part was when everyone got to eat it. Snow ice cream isn't what we know as ice cream. It's more like a milkshake. Sugar was heavily rationed and wasn't included.

"We gathered snow and just added a few ingredients that were available." Crazy enough, just mixing clean snow with a few ingredients such as vanilla and any type of milk, creating a delicious treat.

"When it snowed, we got to stay home from school." Growing up in Southern California, I know nothing about snow days and am very jealous. "And along with staying home from school, we had snow ice cream. We played lots of games to entertain ourselves, but the big entertainment was always the snow ice cream. It was something we always did and loved it when it snowed. We have always been a close family and always did what our parents did when they were children. They grew up with snow ice cream, and so they grew up teaching their children about it."

It was a special event in her life since each generation passed it along. Cindy carried on the family tradition and made snow ice cream for her two boys, one of which is my husband, Rod. So, I asked him about it.

"What I remember the most was using Nestle quick over the snow. My mom would say, 'Boys, it's snowing,' and we knew we could make snow ice cream. It was really like a chocolate slushy. As a kid getting to eat that was great. You had to be real careful about the first snow because there could be a lot of dirt in it. My mom made a big deal about it because it was exciting and fun. And it was fun for me when I was a kid."

Cindy went on with her own childhood memories, "Snow ice cream was something that was made for the little kids so they can get excited about it. When we were really little, we were given an old wooden spoon to stir the ice cream so we could help make it. That's just the way they did things back then."

As the kids got older, they taught the incoming young children how to make it. It was a favorite tradition passed down in the family.

"Mom would have everyone go get something to make it. 'You go get the bowls; you go get the white snow' things, like that. The little ones would watch and would start to help as they got older." She reminisces fondly.

The other fun part about eating snow ice cream for Cindy was playing cards. "The card game we played was called hell." Which is a word I was very surprised to hear her say. She was very religious. "When all the cards were gone, you would yell 'hell!'. Whoever said hell was the winner. We also played a game called spoons. Whoever wound up with the most spoons won."

Cindy didn't remember the details of either game; however, she remembered the fun of playing them while eating snow ice cream. It was all part of the big, imagined world created by her grandma during World War II.

"You just don't know what you are missing when you are having fun."

If you live in a part of the country where it snows, try making snow ice cream. It is easy and delicious. Kids will absolutely love the process as well as the eating. Just don't forget, no yellow snow.

SNOW ICE CREAM

This is meant to be of a milkshake consistency. How many servings it will make depends entirely on the size of your serving bowl/cup and how fast the snow melts. The good thing is that if it's snowing, you can always make more!

INGREDIENTS:

- 8-10 Cups Snow (Make sure it's the second snow and not yellow)
- Quantity as needed (see directions) Any kind of cold milk (cream, evaporated milk, whole milk – cream is best)
- 1 tablespoon vanilla

DIRECTIONS:

1. Put the snow in a large bowl and start adding the milk a little at a time until you get the consistency of a milkshake.
2. Add the vanilla, give it a stir.
3. Enjoy!

CHARLENE'S STORY

"Anyone who's a chef, who loves food, ultimately knows that all that matters is: 'Is it good? Does it give pleasure?'"

—ANTHONY BOURDAIN

CHARLENE HUNN—THE STORY OF SIMPLICITY AT ITS FINEST AND A VERY INSPIRING GRANDMA

Age 37, Mom/Chef/Creator of Chef Adventures on YouTube

I've known Charlene and her husband Jason for about two years now. We met through our YouTube cooking community. She is just adorable, and we became fast friends. On her channel, Chef Adventures, Charlene's moniker is "Hot Chef." Chef Adventures is a husband and wife team with a huge passion for their field.

"We have thirty-two years of combined industrial cooking and high-volume restaurant experience. We explore the awesome world of the culinary arts, amazing food, incredible cooking techniques. Educational and entertaining!"

Even though they are in Florida and I am in Idaho, we have happy hours online as often as our busy schedules allow.

Charlene has been working professionally as a chef for nineteen years. Back when she was in school deciding that there was nothing she would rather do more than cook, she watched the Food Network all the time.

"They made it seem that a chef's life was so glamorous, but it's actually not," she tells me, almost mid-laugh. "It's a lot of hard work, yet I love it. And I will never stop."

Charlene was in the eighth grade when she decided she wanted to cook for a living. She knew she wouldn't want to do anything else. She took all the home economic classes, reading as many cookbooks as she could. Back then, there were actually cooking classes in school. She won Food Service Student of the Year for 2001. After graduating high school, she went to a technical college for culinary arts right away.

The biggest influence on Charlene's love of cooking was her maternal grandmother, "Nana" Catherine.

"My grandma is the reason I decided I wanted to cook for my profession." Catherine is an excellent cook and loves to cook from scratch. "I have many cherished memories in her kitchen. She used to host lots of parties, and I always used to help her cook."

Catherine is American but has an Italian accent. She was born in the United States, later moving to Sicily during World War II due to some immigration issues when she was three years old. Her mom was Italian, and her dad was American. She actually forgot how to speak English living in Italy at such a young age and had to relearn it when she returned to the states.

When Charlene was young, her grandmother watched her and her two younger brothers while her parents were working. They lived next door to each other. Catherine would pick them up from the bus stop and take care of them until their parents came home. Charlene and her brothers would spend the day with their grandmother during the summers, and those memories are clearly lasting a lifetime.

Charlene had a tough time deciding on what recipe to choose for her childhood memory, as many other stories in this book reflect. Eighteen years of childhood food memories provide so many options from which to choose. In Charlene's case, there are even more options than usual. "There are so many recipes because we're Italian." The one she did decide on was quite unexpected.

Charlene's chosen dish from her childhood stems from many visits to Nana's. It is something Catherine always made for them, and it's not Italian. The one dish that brings her back to her childhood is a warm egg salad sandwich. I was as surprised as you are; I was expecting some sort of pasta, but nope, this is her dish, this is her memory.

A fun fact is that Charlene and her husband Jason raise chickens at their home. With chickens come fresh eggs, which — if you haven't had them — are so vastly different from the eggs you buy at the market. The flavors are much richer. Since they usually have an abundance of fresh eggs, this convenience leads perfectly to her childhood dish — her egg salad is made from fresh eggs. Not all of us are as fortunate to have these eggs in our backyard, so we can resort to market eggs.

Charlene describes the egg salad sandwich as "So simple, so delicious, so good." Her grandmother reserved this dish for the summertime visits, which made it all the more special.

"Summers with her were the most fun. It was just one of the many beautiful dishes she used to feed us. She never really made it for us after school, only during the summers because we were with her all day. After school, she used to watch us only for a little while before my Mom came home."

When Charlene was little, this was a dish she looked forward to. "Warm egg salad sandwich on white bread was one of my favorite things. It still is. It was served to me as a scoop of egg salad on one slice of bread folded in half. They used to fill us up, and then we used to watch Matlock, a 1980s American mystery legal drama starring Andy Griffith, in the afternoon."

When she was little, she used to help her grandma by chopping up the eggs. Everything about this simple sandwich makes Charlene extremely happy. She was smiling throughout the entire interview while telling her story, and as she shared the details of this dish, I could visualize these special moments from her childhood.

Charlene actually has egg salad sandwiches on her menu at work and still uses her grandmother's recipe, but now it is served cold. During our interview, talking about it got her craving it.

"Today, I crave those sandwiches. There are literally times when I must have egg salad. Nothing else will do. And no one else's either. I can only eat my own egg salad."

I don't doubt warm egg salad sandwiches were on the dinner table that evening following our interview.

"Recently, I was talking to my grandma. I told her that I was going to make egg salad since we had numerous eggs from our chickens." She makes lunch for Jason when he comes home from work. What a great wife.

While on the phone, Catherine said, "That's a good idea! I have two eggs in my refrigerator, I'm going to make some too!" We've always had this "egg salad connection."

I did ask her if her Nana made up the recipe, and the answer was a heartfelt "Yes."

So with that, here is Catherine's egg salad recipe. Tried and true. Simple. Perfect. Time for lunch — and you don't need to wait for summer to enjoy it.

NANA CATHERINE'S WARM EGG SALAD SANDWICH

INGREDIENTS:
- 1 dozen eggs
- 1 cup mayonnaise
- 2 tablespoons yellow mustard
- 1 teaspoon salt (more or less to taste)
- 1 teaspoon black pepper (more or less to taste)
- Fresh white bread

DIRECTIONS:
1. Boil the eggs for 17 minutes and peel, do not let the eggs cool down.
2. Place in bowl and mash eggs with a whisk to produce a chunky consistency.
3. Add the mayo, mustard, salt, and pepper.
4. Mix until everything is incorporated.
5. Serve immediately on white bread.
6. Enjoy!

JASON'S STORY

"Food is the most primitive form of comfort."

—SHEILAH GRAHAM WESTBROOK

JASON HUNN—THE STORY OF THE FROZEN TUNDRA AND AN INVENTIVE DAD

Age 40, Sous Chef

Jason is the other half of the YouTube channel, Chef Adventures. Jason presents all the grilling and cocktail episodes, alongside many other dishes. One of my favorite episodes is when he created the Drunken Pumpkin Pie Shots. He hollowed out a pumpkin and put a tap into it—creating a pumpkin keg of sorts. He proceeded to pour the shot mixture into the pumpkin and served it from the spout.

His recipes are simple and creative. Between him and Charlene, their channel is fun to watch. I adore this couple. It's beautiful to see how much they truly love each other. They are genuine people, and I am honored to call them friends.

Outside of the channel, Jason is a professional chef. He has the forces of Mother Nature to thank for sending him on this career path.

He lived in Minnesota until he was about twenty-seven. Around 2006, some of his friends that were in his heavy metal band at the time moved down to Florida to chase hurricanes and do storm renovations. They were taking a break from the band. At the time, there was a category four storm, Hurricane Charlie, that ripped the town up that Jason lives in today. His friends were down in Florida working for about a year, and during the whole time, they continued to tell him to move down with them.

After a year, he didn't have anything holding him back, so he decided to make the move to Florida. Their work was winding down, with only about four or five months left. Once that last month hit, his friends moved to Texas for another job, but Jason decided to stay. Good thing he did since he was about to meet the love of his life. He got a job working as a dishwasher in a retirement center. Not the most glamorous occupation; however, he worked hard and got noticed. From there, he started doing food prep and assisting in any way he could.

Jason was doing great work, so much so that the chef at the time, Chef Ron, took him out of the food prep role, put a knife in his hand, and promoted him from prep cook to night cook. That is when he started to develop a true passion for cooking and was on his way to becoming a chef. Charlene happened to work in the kitchen as well.

"She taught me how to cook, how to understand culinary techniques on a professional basis, and how industrial kitchens work."

And that is how they met. Does it get any better?

Jason's childhood food memory comes way before he met his wife. Way before he decided to become a chef. Back when he was a very little boy living in the frozen tundra known more commonly as Minnesota. They moved sixty to seventy miles away from Minneapolis and their families to a remote area. Although this was a charming place, his mother said it was time to move when he was three. Years later, Jason went back and visited that house as an adult, realizing just how brave his parents were for moving away from family and their support system.

When Jason was deciding on his one dish that brings him back to his childhood, he was going back and forth between a dish his mom made and one his dad made. Each of them made dishes that stood out to him. He finally decided that the one dish that brought him back was his dad's mashed potatoes and hamburger gravy, which Jason describes as being "so simple and good." His earliest memory of having this special dish is from when he was about eight years old.

Regular meals consisted of uncomplicated dishes such as grilled cheese, frozen lasagna, and mac and cheese. When Jason's dad, Steve, made his signature dish, he made huge batches in a big chili soup pot. Jason describes it as a big chili-like gravy full of ground beef, onions, and celery. While Jason was between the ages of eight and ten, he vividly remembers his excitement for the dish, eating it up every time. There was something about the celery that he just loved. His animation and happiness, while he described this dish during our interview, were loads of fun to see.

"Big heaping piles of mashed potatoes, big heaping piles of the hamburger gravy over it. I remember getting so full, and it would just sit with you like a rock. And in that frozen tundra, it kept you warm, and it was the most comforting food you could ask for."

It's the perfect winter dish. Minnesota is cold. According to the 2019 article from the Minnesota Department of Natural Resources, "Minnesota's All-Time Record Low," the average winter high is twenty-four degrees Fahrenheit, and the low is ten degrees. As cold as that is, the record low for Minnesota was in 1996, coming in at negative sixty degrees. Just leaving the house was an ordeal. Meals that warm you up from the outside-in are beyond welcome and necessary.

This is his dad's version of a hamburger gravy, that will forever live as one of Jason's favorite meals. "As far as I'm concerned, this is my dad's version of an unknown recipe…and it's delicious." I find it beautiful that this dish has been passed down from father to son.

Jason still makes it two or three times a year without putting his chefy spin on it, not even updating it with real mashed potatoes. Yes, the dish is made with instant mashed potatoes, and "that is the way it must be." This is his dish; this is his memory. He sticks to the original recipe, exactly like his dad made it — and you should too. This is pure comfort food.

DAD'S HAMBURGER GRAVY

INGREDIENTS:
- 2 stalks of celery, diced
- 1 onion, diced
- 2 lbs. ground beef
- 3 packets brown gravy mix (located in the spice aisle of most markets)
- 1 tablespoon salt
- 2 teaspoons pepper
- 1 tablespoon granulated garlic
- 1 box instant mashed potatoes

DIRECTIONS:
1. Prepare the mashed potatoes according to the instructions on the box, set to the side.
2. Cook onion, celery, and ground beef in a large saucepan over medium heat until onion and celery have softened.
3. Continue cooking, and when the beef has cooked throughout, drain the fat from pan.
4. Make the brown gravy packets according to package directions.
5. Once gravy is finished, pour it over the ground beef, mix everything together on medium heat.
6. When gravy has thickened, place mashed potatoes on a plate or bowl, pour hamburger gravy over top of potatoes.
7. Enjoy!

VANESSA'S STORY

"When you hang out with laggers, you'll never be on time for the appetizers."

—CHARMAINE J. FORDE

VANESSA COLE—THE STORY OF ROVING BOAT PARTIES AND THE WACKY CAST OF CHARACTERS
Age 62, Historian/Genealogist

Vanessa is a genealogist—a person who traces family ancestry. She does fascinating work, helping people travel back in time to discover their personal history, uncovering the stories behind who they are. I resonate with this since, once again, your past defines who you are now. I talk about food from childhood, and Vanessa talks about generations of the past. Both roads lead to self-discovery. Vanessa's story goes back to my favorite decade, the 1970s, which is always my favorite thing.

Her story took place in the very early 1970s, when she was thirteen years old. Her family had a 1962 forty-five-foot Chris Craft Constellation, named the Fox Corpen, in Virginia Beach, Virginia. It was an absolutely stunning boat with a wood deck, two bedrooms, two bathrooms, a kitchen, and plenty of living space both inside and out, perfect for Vanessa's family. I know you are curious as to where the name, Fox Corpen, came from. The previous boat owner was Mike Christian, a Navy pilot. He was one of the men held in prison during Vietnam with John McCain. The conditions were horrific, and the men faced starvation and torture during their five-and-a-half years of imprisonment. Mike named the boat; it was originally supposed to be named "The Foxtrot Corpen." When it was time to paint the name on, the "trot" was left out. Mike decided not to worry about it, so "Fox Corpen" it was. Vanessa's family decided to keep the name to honor him for his service and what he had been through. So beautiful.

The boat was perfect for sea travel. Vanessa and her brother shared the forward bedroom, which had bunk beds, and her parents had the aft, or back, stateroom, which was a full bedroom. The family lived on the boat for most of the year. Vanessa mentioned they lived on the boat more days out of the year than their house in Northern Virginia. She attended school in her hometown; however, every weekend, Holiday, and the entire summer was spent on the water. They did not return home until Labor Day. This was a huge part of her life and childhood memory.

"These were the most amazing memories and the most amazing people. I will never forget some of these people. That's what strikes me with these memories."

Initially, the boat was docked at a motel marina which simply means there was a motel at the marina. The motel has since been replaced with condos. All the big boats, including theirs, were parallel parked at one end, and all the smaller boats were at the other end where they could back in. And it's within these parked boats that our story and cast come to life.

Behind Vanessa's family boat were the Osmonds. Sorry, no relation to Donny and Marie. Husband Jack was just a happy-go-lucky, wonderful, fun guy. His wife Jean would be known today as "Miss thing." When Vanessa told me about Jean, she played the part. She twisted her hair and changed her voice to sound like a very distraught southern belle. It was a wonderful impression. Jean always had a problem and needed to share it with everyone, and it was hilarious. One day poor Jean's bra was just too tight, and she needed to let everyone know. "My bra is too tight; I've got to get another one." Vanessa loved her, but she was a character.

Her other next-door neighbors were the Wileys.

"Ben and Martha Wiley were opposites in many ways. He was quiet and had a very dry sense of humor. He didn't say a whole lot, but when he did, it was funny. He always had a drink in his hand; of course, so did EVERYBODY else. Martha never stopped talking! I mean never. She was from North Carolina and had a very southern accent. Where he was reserved, she was never-ending energy and never stopped."

In front of them was the Jacobsons, who were a lovely family.

"Buddy and Nancy Jacobson were always warm and welcoming." She remarked, "They had the largest boat, and many times we all ended up on it in what became an impromptu potluck supper. I remember going back to our boat and helping my mom throw something together and then heading back down the dock with it to share with everyone. My mom had a cookbook for quick and easy semi-homemade recipes, and she always had ingredients ready to do something out of that cookbook."

I collect vintage cookbooks, and most of the recipes I share on my channel come from them. You just never know what you are going to find when you acquire a new vintage cookbook and start reading. They are absolute treasures, and I can see how a semi-homemade cookbook would be perfect for these days on the boat.

The Jacobson's parked their boat closest to the motel's dining room. It was common for people who had too many cocktails to stumble out of the dining room and come on to their boat, sit on the deck and pretend they were the boat owners.

"The Jacobsons would show up and have to say, 'excuse me, this is not your boat, this is our boat, and you have to leave now,'" Vanessa laughed while sharing this. "This was in the 1970s before a time when you ran to court for trespassing. You just took care of it."

It happened so often; the friends couldn't leave that alone. One time Vanessa's parents and the Wileys got on the boat before the Jacobsons showed up to pretend they were drunk visitors. Just good friends, having fun.

These are the people who fill Vanessa's memories and who make the foods we'll be talking about special.

The roving boat parties stick out to her the most, creating her childhood memory. These parties, which happened every weekend during this time, were BYOB (Bring Your Own Booze), and everyone would bring appetizers to share. Vanessa's favorite two appetizers were her mom's pineapple cheese ball and her sausage balls. She and her brother would sneak the sausage balls all the time. Who could blame them? They are so good.

The sausage balls are warm and taste like pure perfection. When you bite into one, the melting cheese mixed with the sausage is just heaven. These truly stood the test of time as they are still popular today. It's no wonder why it's one of her favorites. In fact, she still makes these two recipes today.

Cheese balls were popular in the 1970s. They are easy to make, delicious, and the variations are endless. Mixing pineapple and cream cheese — as Vanessa's mom did — creates a party in your mouth. Today, cheese balls are a fun way to celebrate the cocktail parties of the past.

The parties would start in front of the three boats; Vanessa's family, the Osmonds, and the Henrys. Everyone else would walk over from their boats for the first stop. The dock box, which is the storage box attached to the dock, always made a perfect table once a tablecloth was thrown over it. The first three families would put out their appetizers while the boats further down had their appetizers ready to serve on their dock box when the party got to them.

"They would nibble and mingle and drink … and when everyone was done nibbling and mingling and drinking, we moved on down to the Wileys and the Jacobson's boat where the whole thing started all over again. And when that was done, we moved on down the dock to the smaller boats, where they set out their appetizers. Everyone came to all the boats. It truly was a roving boat party."

By the time the parties were done, there was no dinner needed.

Eventually, some of the friends sold their boats. "By that time, it was pretty much just a small group on the boat. We still did the roving parties, but they weren't happening as often as the earlier years."

Vanessa has many wonderful memories about these parties and the cast of characters. Like anything in life, change happens and people go their separate ways. The family eventually moved to the Cavalier Yacht Club. The only friends that moved with them were the Jacobsons, who were on a different dock. The logistics that made the roving boat parties so convenient were gone. The friends still went on cruises together; however, the days of moving down the dock, drink in one hand, appetizer in the other, faded away. The marvelous memories live on with Vanessa.

"These were some of the best years of my life." I loved watching Vanessa tell these stories. She was reliving and all smiles as she shared, knowing how lucky she was to have had these experiences. "If I had one superpower, it would be time travel, and I'd go back to the boat days ... often!"

All grown up with a family of her own, Vanessa makes her favorite sausage balls and pineapple cheese ball every Christmas. Every Christmas is made that more special by bringing back the memories of the boat parties. Today, she makes the sausage balls whenever she is invited to a party and asked to bring something to share. Sometimes the pineapple cheese ball will make an appearance.

Get some 1970s into your life. Even if your best disco bell bottoms and halter tops are long gone, bring some of the past back with these very retro appetizers. Make them and close your eyes. Transport yourself to the boat dock and join the roving boat parties. You know I did!

VANESSA'S MOM'S APPETIZERS

PINEAPPLE CHEESE BALL

INGREDIENTS:
- 2 packages (8 ounces each) cream cheese
- 1 can (20 ounces) crushed pineapple, well-drained
- 3 cups finely chopped pecans, divided
- 1/4 cup finely chopped green pepper
- 1 tablespoon finely chopped onion
- 1 teaspoon seasoned salt
- Assorted crackers

DIRECTIONS:

1. In a large bowl, beat cream cheese until smooth.
2. Stir in pineapple, 1-1/2 cups pecans, green pepper, onion, and seasoned salt.
3. Shape into two balls.
4. Wrap it in plastic; refrigerate for at least 30 minutes.
5. Place remaining pecans in a small shallow bowl; roll cheese balls in pecans to coat evenly.
6. Serve with your favorite crackers.
7. Enjoy!

CLASSIC BISQUICK SAUSAGE BALLS

INGREDIENTS:

- 1 pound pork sausage
- 2 cups Baking Mix (such as Bisquick)
- 16 ounces sharp cheddar cheese, freshly grated (about 4 cups)

DIRECTIONS:

1. Preheat oven to 350F.
2. Line a baking sheet with parchment paper for easy cleanup.
3. In a large mixing bowl, combine the raw sausage, baking mix, and freshly grated cheese.
4. Mix well until the ingredients start to hold together.
5. The mixture should be moist enough that when you squeeze it and roll it into a ball, it will hold its shape instead of crumbling.
6. Use a 2 tablespoons cookie scoop to evenly portion the mixture and roll into approximately golf ball-sized balls.

(if you don't have a cookie scoop, just measure an over-filled soup spoon and roll into balls.)

7. Transfer balls to the lined baking sheet.
8. Bake 22–25 minutes until golden brown and cooked through.
9. Serve hot with toothpicks for skewering and your favorite dipping sauce.
10. Enjoy!

MARGARET'S STORY

"Food is symbolic of love when words are inadequate."

—ALAN D. WOLFELT

MARGARET—THE STORY OF BONFIRE NIGHT AND PARKIN

YouTube Baker

My YouTube creator circle is marvelous. Another person who has become a good friend is Margaret. She lives in the United Kingdom and has a voice I could listen to all day. She bakes amazing goodies on her channel, Margaret's Make and Bake, always stating, "I love making and baking." She shares how to bake tarts, cookies, cakes, and many other scrumptious morsels — every one of them delicious. Some are from her childhood, and some are new.

"My aim is to make following a recipe effortless so you can easily follow. All makes and bakes are simple enough for anyone to master, whatever your previous experience. The ingredients to use are shared at the start of each video so you can get them together before you begin, and making your baking session easy and enjoyable." Every dish she makes will make your mouth water.

Much of this story is from a document Margaret sent to me. I intentionally kept her UK spelling of several words through-out this chapter. I love the spelling, the way it reads, and I feel it takes us back to Margaret's childhood home in England.

"When we were children, we lived in the North of England. It was the early sixties, and Bonfire Night was always big in our house. It was a whole family event."

As National Today tells us in their article, "History of Bonfire Night", the holiday, otherwise known as Guy Fawkes Night, is a big observance primarily in the United Kingdom. This night celebrates the failed attempt to blow up the Houses of Parliament and King James I on November 5, 1605. Guy Fawkes, a member of the Gunpowder Plot, was arrested on that day while guarding the gunpowder, thereby thwarting the plot. Prior to interviewing Margaret, I never knew this holiday existed. I find it fun to learn about holidays in other countries. With holidays comes holiday foods and, of course, childhood memories.

"My mother would do a great deal of baking in the days leading up to the fifth of November." You can see where Margaret got her love of baking. Her mom would have the table set with all the sweets and treats a child could ever want. "There would be crunchy toffee apples, made with the sweet sugar, boiled until it became thick and luscious. Then each apple already planted firmly onto a wooden lollipop stick was dunked into this beautifully sweet, sticky glaze and swirled until completely covered. And there they stood, as straight as soldiers on the baking tray to set."

Some of the other food on her family kitchen table included sausage rolls wrapped in scrumptious homemade puff pastry and sausage meat, which had sweet, caramelized onions added in. With all of the children quite excited, they were kept busy putting together cheese skewers. "These were cheese cubes and mini pickled onions impaled with cocktail sticks, like beads on a thread."

Very smart mom, giving the kids a delicious project to keep their little hands and minds occupied. I remember, as I am sure you do too, as a child, a few hours of waiting can seem like days.

Thus, the food for Bonfire Night continued. "There were chestnuts in a bowl. And then, my very favourite of all, Parkin." Margaret's childhood memory.

Parkin, the much-anticipated treat of the night, required much patience. This treat defined Bonfire Night for her; this is what she waited for. "Parkin was the clear star of the night. A dark sticky cake that included both heavy, strong jet-black treacle as well as light, sweet and sticky golden syrup. Parkin had to be made several days before it was to be eaten, giving it chance to mature, becoming even more sticky. It was at its best five days after baking, and the wait was intolerable."

Margaret's childhood memories were her inspiration to become the wonderful baker she is today.

"We knew when Mother had made it as the kitchen air held its sweet and heavy aroma for several hours afterwards. The cake tin containing this dark delight was always kept up on the highest shelf. She did not want little fingers opening the tin for a smell or a taste. I have the original recipe from mum's old cookbook. It used to include lard, but I find it is much nicer and richer with butter. Parkin was such a lovely treat, it looked a bit like a dark ginger cake, yet it had oatmeal and was made with both golden syrup and black treacle, which made it heavy, dense, dark, and delicious. Its texture was nothing like ginger cake." In America, ginger cake is known as gingerbread.

After coming home from school, Margaret and her siblings had to do what every child hates to do — wait. While they would so badly want to start launching the customary fireworks, the explosives were understandably off limits to little fingers. Instead, "they were kept in the darkroom which housed the coal store in an old and shabby metal tin box which we were under strict instructions never to go anywhere near."

"Father was in his greatcoat preparing the fireworks. The rockets were placed into old-fashioned milk bottles right at the far end of the garden for the Catherine-Wheel." According to the *Oxford Learner's Dictionarie*, a Catherine-Wheel is a round flat firework that turns around in circles when lit. "This was nailed onto the fence, and several of the standing fireworks planted in different areas among the plants to give us a surprise as they exploded into colours."

Her description reminds me of celebrating the Fourth of July in America. The respective meanings behind them are different, of course—but there are still those lasting memories of being a child eagerly waiting for the night sky to light up with explosions of color.

England can be very cold. In fact, I have learned from other friends that live in the United Kingdom that houses normally don't even have air conditioning. I'm still trying to wrap my head around that. With the weather, young children outside at night had to dress very warmly. No one was allowed outside until they were properly and warmly dressed.

When they were finally allowed to go outside, their mom placed a piece of treacle toffee — which is similar to molasses — right into their mouth so it wouldn't stick to their gloves. What a perfect way to start the evening.

With strict instructions to touch the wall at all times to prevent any injury, they watched their father make the final preparations. There were no streetlights, so it was pitch black, but they were able to see their father as he went around the long garden carrying a glowing stick made from stiffened rope to light his way. The toffee kept them occupied during the wait.

Margaret continues, "The giggling and chatting came to an abrupt end as the first rocket exploded into an array of the brightest light, and we all 'oohed and aahed' as each one blasted with a bang and a flash of colour. We then stood on the path with sparklers, drawing in the air with these delightful writing tools. We tried to write our name, but the beginning of the word would fade before we got to the end. I think I managed it once; however, it's very hard to remember, and perhaps I had just wished it so." I remember doing the exact same thing with sparklers. Luckily, my name is short.

All around the world, holidays are celebrated with special foods, traditions, and events. Through a child's eyes, it is pure magic. Holidays bring us back every time, especially when we are grown and have kids of our own. We, as adults, take pride and excitement in sharing our holidays, foods, and traditions with our children and watch the magic in their eyes. It was such a joy to watch my kids experience the holidays when they were young. It made my heart sing, and I bet Margaret's parents felt similarly sharing their traditions.

After the fireworks, it was time to go back to the warmth inside the house. "We were ushered into the kitchen to peel off the layers we had donned for the exercise, and at last, we could taste the beautiful treats that were laid out on the kitchen table for our enjoyment. But not the Parkin; that was for later."

The food was a memorable part of the night's celebrations, and so were the fun games. While in America, bobbing for apples is mainly reserved for Halloween, Margaret and her family would do this as part of Bonfire Night. Sometimes the apples were hung on threads, and other times they were placed in a tin baby bathtub full of water for the kids to grab with their teeth. This was the messier way to play the game, but it was so much fun.

"We gathered round the fireplace where the fire was roaring in the grate. Pleased to be in the warmth after the cold of the winter and the wet of the apple bobbing."

Sitting in front of the fire, it was time for the chestnuts. Margaret's father cooked them in the fireplace for the family. To cook a chestnut properly, he would poke it with a fork and toss it into the fire. Poking it releases the steam so the chestnut won't explode. "That one's ready," he would say as they were sprinkled with salt and passed around.

Finally, it was time for the Parkin, the one dish that brings Margaret right back to her childhood, celebrating Bonfire Night with her family.

"After all the excitement of the evening, we sat with supper, which consisted of hot chocolate and the long-awaited Parkin. As the tin was opened, we could smell the rich treat. Mother sliced it while Father made the hot chocolaty drinks. The creaminess of that warm, thick drink gave a beautiful chocolaty addition to the spicy stickiness of the Parkin. The perfect match, in my opinion."

It had been a while since Margaret experienced her childhood favorite Parkin, until now. "I have not had Parkin since those long-forgotten days, and I made it this week. It was just as lovely as I remembered, with that steaming hot mug of chocolate, of course." Food can bring you right back.

Margaret has a Parkin video on her channel where you can watch her make it and listen to her lovely voice. I am so honored that she shared her childhood memories with me. It is clear why Parkin is so special to her. Sometimes the details are fuzzy, yet the emotion is there. Or sometimes, like Margaret, you remember every detail, and you can transport yourself back to those wonderful nights in the 1960s celebrating Bonfire Night.

As Margaret is in the United Kingdom, I have converted her measurements to standard and suggested American ingredients to replace what may not be available in the United States. If you do have the ingredients, by all means, use them. As Margaret shared, this is not her Mom's recipe. This is what she uses now and feels it's much nicer. With Parkin, patience is truly a virtue. Your reward will be a delectable, sticky, and sweet cake, or "pudding," as it is known in the United Kingdom. Happy Bonfire Night!

MARGARET'S PARKIN

Margaret suggests enjoying your Parkin with a steaming mug of hot chocolate, just like she did.

INGREDIENTS:

- 115g (1/2 cup) butter
- 115g (6 tablespoons) golden syrup (honey, do not use corn syrup)

- 2 tablespoons treacle (black strap molasses)
- 140g (3/4 Cup) brown sugar
- 2 teaspoon ground ginger
- 1 teaspoon mixed spice
- 170g (3/4 cup) plain flour
- 1 teaspoon bicarbonate of soda (baking soda)
- 170g (3/4 cup) oatmeal
- 6 tablespoons milk

DIRECTIONS:

1. Preheat oven to 150C or 300F.
2. Butter and line a 9-inch-round cake tin (cake pan) with baking paper.
3. Melt the sugar, butter, golden syrup, and treacle in a pan in a saucepan over low heat.
4. In a bowl, sift the dry ingredients and mix in the oatmeal.
5. Next, stir liquid ingredients in and mix until it's all combined.
6. Pour batter into the prepared tin and bake for 1 hour and 15 minutes.
7. Allow cake to cool completely in the tin, then remove.
8. Wrap the Parkin in waxed paper. Store in an airtight container with a good sealing lid and leave for five days
9. Enjoy!

PATRICK'S STORY

—

"In the childhood memories of every good cook, there's a large kitchen, a warm stove, a simmering pot, and a mom."

—BARBARA COSTIKYAN

PATRICK CARROLL—THE STORY OF AN EMBRACING COMMUNITY AND MUM

Age 50, YouTube Creator

Patrick is very close to his "mum," Maureen, and this story is a tribute to her. Maureen left Scotland for Australia by boat all by herself when she was only sixteen. She lived in poverty in Glasgow and wanted a better life; she now holds a PhD in education. Patrick's father, Alf, followed her about a year or so later. They were childhood sweethearts and married in Australia. At the time, immigrants were coming to Australia from all over Europe searching for that same better life.

Australia was the land of opportunity with many possibilities for work and to raise a family.

Patrick's channel on YouTube is called Paddy Joe Cooking. He was born and raised in Melbourne, Australia, and has the beautiful accent to match. He always starts his shows with "G'day folks…." One of the highlights of Patrick's channel is that he loves to receive gifts of American foods from friends and fans to try on camera. Foods we don't think twice about are new to him, and it's fun to watch him experience them for the first time. What he does next is even more entertaining. He makes up very out-of-the-box recipes using these new-found foods. In other episodes, we get to see over-the-top dishes he creates that include the wonderful ingredients he has in Australia. He is the nicest guy, and it's such a pleasure to call him my friend.

Before our interview, he called his mom to ask about some of the dishes from his childhood. "I was expecting her to say, we did this, or we did that, but she got so excited talking about it. I was amazed at what it brought out in her, and the memories she had were razor sharp. She really got excited about it; I couldn't believe it."

That is the hippocampus in action. Just the suggestion of talking about family dishes of the past took her right back to her kitchen, having young children and making them dinner. Patrick remembered his childhood dinners, and to any mom — yours truly included — that is one of the best things to hear. No wonder she got excited.

Patrick is a first-generation Australian. When he came along, they lived in a semi-rural community near Mount Dandenong in Victoria. The family was very involved in the Catholic Church, which had a large supportive community. His family still maintains friendships from that community to this day.

"There was always cooking for get-togethers. There was a great sense of community." Growing up in that was very memorable. "I had many 'Aunties' and 'Uncles' that were not by blood, but were really close friends. I had great childhood memories, and food was a big part of it."

It was the 1970s, and Patrick was around eight or ten years old. "Back then the food was a big part of our life. And it was comfort food." Food brings us back to that feeling of love and comfort, like a big hug. That is no surprise. Comfort is childhood, and childhood is comfort — this is a big reason why we return mentally to our childhood.

I asked Patrick what the popular dishes were in Australia back in the 1970s when he was growing up.

"Australia is basically an odd place for food. Only in the past ten or fifteen years have we started our own identity with food. We were getting a lot of the recipes from America, so we had similar recipes in the 1970s and 1980s."

This meant large delicious casseroles that were easy to prepare, utilizing the convenience food of the day. In the 1970s, convenience food was still as popular as the 50s and 60s.

"Australia is known for its barbecuing," 'on the barbie' as often quoted, "and there really is a big barbecue culture here. But it's very basic, such as sausages, chops, steaks, that sort of thing. Back then, we weren't into the rubs or smokes. That is happening now, yet it wasn't back then."

The rumors are true; however, they did, and still do, drink a lot of beer. And yes, if you have heard tales, Foster's beer was a thing back then.

Patrick considered many dishes when deciding on his favorite. He has memories of huge casseroles, which meant leftovers for the next day — always a good thing. He considered ground beef — which is referred to as "mince" in Australia and many other European countries—cooked with potatoes, turnips, peas, and gravy. It was very much a peasant dish. Patrick recalls that his "father loved it just over buttered toast."

"As a kid, I didn't do much cooking because my mum was very into it. Yet there has always been an interest. I've worked in catering and have done a lot of hospitality work over the years." Patrick has a big respect for food.

That is no surprise when you learn how much his mom inspired him with her love of cooking. It was a daily event to see her cooking in the kitchen. He saw the delicious meals that came to the table as a result of her work in the kitchen. He saw the ingredients and watched what his mom did to turn them into something indulging. I asked him if that is what inspired him to start his cooking channel. There had to be a connection. However, his start was sort of backward;

Patrick decided to start a channel first and then decide what it would be about after the fact. But the obvious choice was cooking, thanks to the inspiration of his mom. "My mum is amazing."

This is where Patrick's childhood food memory comes in, his mom made many different dishes at all the family meals, potlucks, and church events he attended as a child. "The one dish that keeps coming to my mind is apricot chicken. I remember helping her make it because it was so easy. We would have it regularly, and we all loved the salty-sweet combination. I suppose also since it was so easy to throw together with simple ingredients. I know my father really loved it from the sweetness of the dish; he had such a sweet tooth."

"In addition to apricot chicken, my dad also loved grilled cheese sandwiches or, as he would call it, toasted cheese. He would often have a toasted cheese sandwich for lunch with cups of tea. The day after his birthday, I decided to make my dad a toasted cheese sandwich and added some of the apricot chicken to the sandwich."

I love when kids make up dishes, they can be so inventive. I know I came up with some wild ones.

"My mother recalls that she was quite surprised by my suggestion to do this. Once again, with the assistance of my mother, I made this apricot chicken toasted cheese for dad, and he absolutely enjoyed it! He even asked for a second one, apparently."

A new dish was born in Patrick's house. A dish created by a child with an imagination. This story led Patrick down memory lane and sparked all sorts of other delightful memories of his dad. All of this was because he was asked about the one dish that brought him back to his childhood.

"I think this book is such a wonderful idea. Food and memories, so often linked and so very precious." Patrick, you cannot be more correct.

Apricot chicken brings comfort, love, and a sense of family — that is why this dish takes Patrick right back to his dinner table in Australia in the 1970s. Sometimes simplicity wins when cooking. Here is Maureen's recipe, just as fabulous now as it was back then.

PATRICK'S MUM'S APRICOT CHICKEN

INGREDIENTS:
- 1 rotisserie chicken, remove skin and bones, then shred meat
- 1 can apricot nectar (these are usually 11.5 oz)
- 1 envelope onion soup mix

DIRECTIONS:
1. Simply mix all ingredients together in a casserole dish and bake on 350F for about 15-20 minutes until warmed through.
2. Serve with mashed potatoes or rice and whatever vegetable you have on hand.
3. Enjoy!

MAX'S STORY

———

"To me, food is as much about the moment, the occasion, the location and the company as it is about the taste."

—HESTON BLUMENTHAL

MAX MILLER–THE STORY OF THE CHUTNEY CHEESE BALL AND CHRISTMAS
Age: 38 — YouTube Creator

The YouTube channel Tasting History with Max Miller just passed one million subscribers, and I am so happy for my friend. I was excited to meet another food history nerd like me. The history his videos explore goes back hundreds of years, highlighting dishes made before stoves and refrigerators. He also uses spices and ingredients that are no longer common. I love to go back in time to discover foods of the past in my videos; however, my "'past" is considered pretty recent compared to Max's 'past.' "Love food? Can't get enough of history? Then you've come to the right place," says Max about his channel, and his fans certainly agree.

As Max has a very successful food channel, I first asked him where he learned to cook.

"My mom would teach me things, but I really wasn't interested in cooking growing up. I was interested in eating," he explained.

"I went on vacation with my friend Maureen to Disneyworld in December of 2015, and she got sick. So, we spent the majority of our vacation in the hotel room. We watched a lot of TV, and she introduced me to *The Great British Bake-Off*." They binge-watched all of season one, "There was something about it. Something so charming and so English; I fell in love with it." Prior to watching that, the only baking Max did came out of a pre-made mix.

"When I came home from my trip, I decided to remake everything I saw on that show, and so I did." He really made everything, all thirty bakes; he started with a Battenburg cake, which was very complicated. He embraced tutorials on baking. "If I'd know how difficult it would be, I probably wouldn't have chosen that first. However, I'm glad that I did because it forced me to learn a lot of techniques really quickly."

Shortly after that, Max started his channel, gaining a huge following quickly. He shared that doing the channel has made him a better cook." I actually prefer baking over cooking. I like a very precise recipe to follow."

Max had a tough time picking the one recipe from his childhood, which was spent in Phoenix, Arizona.

"There was a sausage bread that we would eat every single Christmas Eve that my dad, Tim, used to make. There was a coffee cake that my mom, Pam, makes every Christmas morning, which was not the best coffee cake. One year she tried to improve it. In a way, it was better, but we all told her to go back to the one that takes us back to when we were five years old."

There it is. If we have happy childhood food memories, we want to return to them; they bring us joy.

Max contemplated sharing other dishes. His grandmother's spinach enchilada recipe was also a favorite. His great aunt's monkey bread, "Which wasn't sweet, more buttery, than the one most people know. Now, my brother makes it every single Christmas and is even starting to have his ten-year-old daughter make it." The dishes that moved from generation to generation, and the family traditions that accompany them, are the ones we love to return to as adults.

"The dish I ended up choosing, spanning over my entire life, is a chutney cheese ball. So basically, it's just a ball of cream cheese with spices, and mango chutney poured over it. Really simple, but it was present in every major event in my life. My mom would always make it for Christmas Eve. Whenever we would have a big meal at our house, my mom had appetizers out beforehand, and this was always one of them. It was always present."

No matter the family occasion, be it holidays, graduation, or birthdays — the beloved cheese ball was always there, always waiting at the appetizer table.

"This dish isn't just for Christmas and Easter. It reminds me of my middle school graduation, my high school graduation, my brother's wedding, which was at the house."

I like her style. I love all things appetizers. There is something inviting about arriving at a house for a meal or event, and as you walk in the door, you are greeted with a scrumptious snackable food display. Appetizer possibilities are endless. They can be as easy as a bowl of nuts and the classic onion dip to Swedish meatballs or, my favorite, something out of the 1970s. I love to make retro appetizers on my channel. It is such a great and delicious custom, and every family has their special ones that always make an appearance, such as Max's Chutney Cheese Ball. They just make people feel special as if to say, "I'm glad you're here."

"Every time I taste it, it takes me back to having twenty people in the house. My cousins are there; my grandparents are still alive. Everyone is there leading up to whatever the big event is." Isn't it fascinating that one little appetizer can do so much?

I asked if she had concocted the recipe herself. "I don't know where she got it. I'm sure she got it from some Cooks Illustrated, and then it just changed over the years. It's definitely her version now, though ... when I was a kid, I didn't like it because it was too spicy for me. I think my mom ended up tweaking the recipe to better fit the kids."

But even before Max learned to love the chutney ball, the smell of it was already making positive memories in his mind.

"I have this memory of my parents having friends over before going out. We were going to be at home with the babysitter. She would wear this leather jacket and make this cheese ball. This was back before I liked it, but the scents of the leather jacket, the chutney, and her White Diamonds perfume all together, I think of that, and I am four years old. It's one of my earliest memories, and there is always food connected to those early memories." As we talked about earlier, something's scent is a far greater memory trigger than taste.

This memorable dish was always a last-minute thing that she put together. "It tastes like it should have taken a long time to make, yet it takes like five minutes." His parents would spend all day making the rest of the food, and then about fifteen minutes before people were due at the house, it was crunch time. "I need to get the appetizers out!" Max's mom would say. Suddenly she was directing the family to help slice cheese. Others were told to get plates, crackers and everything else that was needed. "Then she would quickly whisk up the chutney ball." There were even specific dishes used to serve it, as Max describes, "an orangish southwestern-y looking dish or a dish shaped like a turkey." The chutney ball went right into the middle and was one of the first things people ate.

Family traditions are happiness and memories, more than just a holiday or birthday. They go deeper. They are the guest list. They are the game you know you will play. They are a cheese ball. They are love.

"One of the cool things about it is this is one of the first dishes my mom passed off. She gave it to my sister, Caitlin, basically saying, 'Now when we have the holidays, you make this. You bring it over.'" The cheese ball needed to be part of every celebration; it was expected. "To this day, my sister brings over all the ingredients and whisks it up quickly before everyone arrives. And we still have it for every gathering." The cheese ball has now moved to the next generation.

A few years ago, Caitlin was trying to think of things to get Max for Christmas. It was a lean year financially. She asked Max what he wanted, and he knew things were tight. Max knew exactly what he wanted, "I want that chutney cheese ball recipe." With that, she was inspired to make him a very special gift. She made him a recipe box.

"Not only did it have the recipe for the cheese ball nicely written on a card, but she talked to our family and went through old recipes from our grandparents that we had eaten together when we were kids. She pulled together about fifteen of those family recipes. It was one of the best Christmas gifts I've ever gotten." Max received his family food history for Christmas. Kudos to Caitlin.

The humble cheese ball isn't so humble after all. It's memories, heritage, love, and so much more. Here is the recipe — from Max's recipe box to your kitchen.

CREAM CHEESE CHUTNEY CHEESE BALL

INGREDIENTS:
- 8-ounce package softened cream cheese
- 2 dashes of Tabasco sauce
- A large pinch of garlic powder
- 2 teaspoons curry powder
- 2 teaspoons worcestershire sauce
- 1 cup mango chutney — Max says, "Trader Joe's has the perfect chutney for this recipe" (or use your favorite)

DIRECTIONS:
1. Beat the cream cheese in a medium bowl until smooth.
2. Add the Tabasco, garlic powder, curry powder, and Worcestershire sauce and mix until incorporated.
3. Refrigerate for 30 minutes.
4. With large spoons or your hands, form the mixture into a large ball and set in a serving dish.
5. Pour the mango chutney over the top.
6. Serve with toast or crackers.
7. Enjoy!

ASHLEY'S STORY

"Food brings people together on many different levels. It's nourishment of the soul and body; it's truly love."

—GIADA DE LAURENTIIS

ASHLEY DEPAS—THE STORY OF A SUPERWOMAN AND HER CHILI CHEESE CASSEROLE

Age: Mature Adult, Dog Mom/ Flower Lover/ Wife

Working at Guitar Center over ten years ago, I met Ashley, and we became instant friends. We got to know each other over many lunches, coffee breaks, and walks. She is a compassionate animal lover, fighting for the title of "Best Dog Mom", and a big flower enthusiast. We both adore Disneyland — where they have amazing flowers — and have been trying to go together for years. We haven't made it yet, but I hold out hope that one day we will.

Ashley grew up in Canoga Park, California, in the 1970s. At that time, this area was a beautiful suburb of Los Angeles. The weather was always great, with green trees against blue skies. If there are clouds, they are sprinkled along the view. There is a joke that Southern California is a "dry heat." It's very true, and my curly hair can testify to that. When there is an ounce of humidity, hair turns to frizz. When I lived in Southern California, most days were great hair days. No humidity, which is the dry heat everyone often referred to. So, when you see the Brady Bunch on reruns, and they are playing in their pretend backyard on a beautiful day, the chances are that it truly was a beautiful day in real life. Funny enough, the outside shot of the "Brady Bunch" house used in the show is only about twenty minutes from Canoga Park.

"If you think about the Brady Bunch, that is the kind of neighborhood I grew up in." laughed Ashley.

Ashley's parents both worked. "My mom was a nurse, and my dad worked for a brewery in inventory control."

"I had a very good childhood. I'm very lucky." Ashley is the youngest of six. "We all got along. My parents just wanted us to be happy and good people. Look after your siblings, look after your neighbors, be kind to people, do your best."

Knowing Ashley, I can now fully see her upbringing within her after learning this. She is such a kind and good-hearted person; her parents did a wonderful job. I asked her if she is still close with all of her siblings, and I received the answer I expected: "Yes, we talk pretty regularly." On a fun note, her oldest brother bought the family home.

"My mom was a superwoman." She had a career and raised six kids. "Very pragmatic, very centered, no freak-outs, like you would picture a nurse to be."

Ashley told one story about her mom that is just fabulous.

"We had property about thirty miles outside of Temecula, CA, and spent a lot of time there as a family. One day, my mom found and killed a rattlesnake on the property. She chopped off its head, skinned it, and cooked it for dinner. I kid you not."

Ashley was about seven when this happened. She tasted it, not knowing what it was, but when she found out, she didn't go back for seconds. Yet this goes to the role model she had in her life — nurse, mom, exterminator of venomous reptiles, and again, superwoman.

Ashley's childhood food memory is simplicity at its finest, Her mom's chili cheese casserole.

"The first time I remember having it, I was around ten. And as an adult, it ticks all the boxes. Stuff you more than likely have in your house, you can easily halve the recipe, you can make it vegetarian, it travels well, it freezes well, it reheats well, it's budget-friendly, it's potluck-friendly, and all that is needed is one bowl and one dish. So, being an adult and reflecting back to being the youngest of six children, it makes sense that my parents would make that since it was simple." Having six kids myself, I know how hectic it can be to feed the whole family after a long day at work. Even a superwoman appreciates a dinner that is delicious but also easy and quick to prepare. This casserole didn't disappoint.

Ashley's mom would make this for the family maybe once a month. "There was always that excitement," when Ashley knew tonight would be the night to have this casserole. "It's warm, it's cheesy, it's got chilies in it. It wasn't spicy, but I felt an 'ooh, fancy' feeling. It was comfort. Actually, I would call it cheesy, creamy comfort." It is quite clear why Ashley chose this as her dish.

"We could also request it if we had everything in the house. This was a 'Hey Mom, can we have chili cheese casserole for dinner tonight' kind of dish. That was a special thing as a child, to be able to request it."

Ashley doesn't know where her mom got the recipe. "It was probably from the church we went to as kids. The congregation had a collaborative cookbook, and I imagine she probably got it from one of those books."

A collaborative cookbook is where everyone in a group contributes recipes to create a local cookbook. I add them to my collection as often as I can and have done several episodes celebrating recipes from families of the past. Talk about memories! They are one of my favorite vintage cookbook styles; you get to peek into families of the past and see what they loved to cook. When these treasured recipes are shared, they are personal. Most of the recipes I've tried, and I've tried more than I can count, are delightful. Today you can look back if your mom or grandma, or dad or grandpa for that matter, contributed to one of these precious books and see their recipe, their piece of history — really, their legacy. These types of cookbooks are pure treasures. No wonder a childhood food memory most likely came from there.

"I also loved this dish because, as kids, we could help make it. One of the things I really liked to do was tear up the tortillas in a way, so they fit perfectly or close to perfectly around the edges of the square dish. Something about lining the edges really well and overlapping them felt like it would make the "filling" more layered. Also, when that can of chili got mixed in, it felt like the absolute ultimate … the light aroma, the color mixed in. A child's concept of south of the border flavors, I suppose."

Today, Ashley is still layering tortillas with chili and cheese, celebrating the warm, cheesy, and oh-so-fancy casserole of her childhood.

"I made it two weeks ago. I don't make it often, maybe twice a year." I asked her if she makes it the same way her mom used to make it or if she adds her own touches. "I DO NOT change a thing…I still make it exactly the way my mom does. I rarely make it at our house, it is usually a special treat that I like to make when I visit my mom." She absolutely loves it; now Ashley is making the dish that her mom made for her.

You know how memorable a childhood dish is when you make it as an adult. The first bite can bring you right back to your family dinner table and your special request. It is pure comfort.

Now you can make it too. An easy dinner in minutes and such a delicious one. Your kids may even start requesting it. Or, even more fun, have your kids help make it. Ashley loved that, and it's fun to get the family involved in making dinner. It sets up some great childhood memories for them. And, rattlesnake is not required.

ASHLEY'S MOM'S CHILI CHEESE CASSEROLE

INGREDIENTS:
- 1 1/4 pounds grated cheddar cheese
- 1 pint of sour cream
- 2 cans of cream of chicken (or cream of mushroom) soup
- 12 corn tortillas
- 1 4 oz can diced green chilies

DIRECTIONS:
1. Combine all ingredients except tortillas in bowl.
2. Spray 9x13 baking dish with cooking spray.
3. Tear* apart six of the tortillas and put in the baking dish.
4. Top with half the mixture.
5. Tear apart the other six tortillas and place on top of the mixture.
6. Top with the rest of the mixture.
7. Bake covered at 350F for 45 minutes.
8. Let rest for 5–10 before serving.
9. Enjoy!

*tear them into about 4/5 pieces. You want them to be small enough to chew but big enough to support the mix.

JIMMY'S STORY

"Food is a gift and should be treated reverentially--romanced and ritualized and seasoned with memory."

—CHRIS BOHJALIAN

JIMMY DICK—THE STORY OF FAMILY REUNIONS AND THE SMELL OF GRANDMA
Age 57, YouTube Creator/Dad/Husband/Author

Jimmy is an author and creates cooking videos as "Jimmy Dick" (a play on his real name) on his YouTube channel, Jimmy Dick's International Kitchen. "Get ready to cook with easy recipes that anyone can master. I have a wide variety of international recipes from all over the world, so get ready to impress whoever you are cooking for. It is my opinion that anyone can cook. I love food from every ethnic background and would love for you to join me on this journey." Jimmy is also an author of three cookbooks, two very funny comedy books, and a horror story. He covers many genres in his writing.

Jimmy grew up in Dayton, Ohio, and then moved to Stanton, Kentucky, when he was sixteen—which was "in the middle of nowhere," according to him. Jimmy believes moving was great for him food-wise because, back in Ohio, he didn't like anything his parents cooked. "Nothing at all."

It's certainly an interesting beginning for a future cookbook author. Many kids are picky eaters, but Jimmy would soon learn in Kentucky to appreciate whatever was served.

In Kentucky, he worked on his brothers-in-law, Bugsy's, tobacco farm where they worked from daybreak to dark. Every day, after a long, hard day of work, they went to Bugsy's mother Nora's house for dinner. "Every night, she would pull out enough food to cover the table. You got what you were served, and that was it." She would say, "'It may not be much, but it will fill your belly.' And I thought, man, this was more than our Thanksgiving dinners at home."

Jimmy went on to realize that "It saved my life in a lot of ways moving away from Ohio. It also gave me a good work ethic, and it made me appreciate food more." Moving to Kentucky taught him the benefit of hard work and the goodness in people that he did not see in Dayton. "Southern hospitality was a real thing. It totally changed the direction of my life. Because of that, I joined the Air Force and spent the next twenty years serving." That is what brought him to Colorado, where he currently lives.

He joined the Air Force when he was nineteen and got to travel the world. "And because I love to eat, I've always said I have a weight problem. I can't wait to eat. I just appreciate food from all over the planet." This is where the inspiration for his international cooking channel came from. He brought something home with him from wherever he traveled. When he came home on leave from the Air Force, his parents and sisters would wait to see what new dish he would make. "So, I had to learn something new to make for them."

His memory to share with us takes him right back to his grandma Eleanor, whose entire career was spent working in a bakery. He was five or six at the time.

"Every time she would hug us, she would smell like cake, and you just wanted to lean in and take in whiffs of grandma since she smelled like a bakery. We had a lot of family reunions growing up in Ohio, which included about thirty kids. Grandma would make the grandkids their favorite pies for their birthdays. She would also make all the wedding cakes for the family."

Jimmy's grandma was an amazing baker all around. However, her cookies were truly delightful. She made Aunt Sally's Cocoa Drops just for him, and they are his favorite. Interestingly enough, the recipe was not hers. "She found this recipe in 1940 on a bag of flour, so we don't know who Aunt Sally is, but they are wonderful."

"I can remember coming home from kindergarten and smelling the delicious smell of cocoa drops. I remember it was fall, and I came in from the crisp fall air that smelled of fallen leaves. So, when I stepped into the front door, I was greeted with warm chocolaty aroma that made me feel safe and loved."

It's a very old-school, scratch recipe with butter and shortening. It is so exceptional to Jimmy; not only is it from his grandma, but the smell reminds him of her. This goes right back to when we talked about how food can be an anchor to your memories, especially the scent. These cookies take Jimmy right back to being a little boy hugging his wonderfully bakery-scented grandma. He makes these cookies to this day, once a year at Christmas.

It's so gratifying to celebrate a childhood memory by sharing it with your family as an adult. Plus, it is such a beautiful way to honor a family member; It brings comfort to your heart. Jimmy always looked forward to and continues to keep the family recipe alive.

The decadent cookies his grandma made are his memories that bring him right back to his childhood. When he talks about his grandma, he smiles. "I will always remember hugging her and smelling sugar. She smelled sweet, and she was."

AUNT SALLY'S COCOA DROPS (GRANDMA'S COOKIES)

INGREDIENTS:
- 1/2 cup shortening
- 1 teaspoon vanilla
- 1/2 cup cocoa
- 1 egg

- 1/2 teaspoon baking soda
- 1 cup sugar
- 3/4 cup buttermilk
- 1/2 teaspoon salt
- 1 3/4 cup flour

DIRECTIONS:

1. Cream (using a hand or stand mixer, mix well until thoroughly combined) shortening, sugar, egg, vanilla, salt, and buttermilk until smooth.
2. Add the remaining ingredients one at a time mixing well until combined.
3. Drop cookie dough by the tablespoon onto ungreased baking sheet (these are drop cookies, no shaping needed), bake at 400F for 8 minutes, the bottom should have very little color.
4. Remove from the baking sheet while still warm and cool on a flat piece of wax paper. (The wax paper is an important step as it allows the cookie to steam from underneath and makes it taste good and fudgy.)
5. "Next" Jimmy advises, "pour yourself a glass of ice-cold milk."
6. Enjoy!

FRENCHY'S STORY

"I will not eat them in a house, I will not eat them with a mouse, I will not eat them in a box, I will not eat them with a fox, I will not eat them here of there, I will not eat them anywhere, I do not like green eggs and ham, I do not like them, Sam-I-Am."

—DR. SEUSS, GREEN EGGS AND HAM

FRENCHY—THE STORY OF THE PERFECT FOOD AND CULINARY PATIENCE

Age 39, Businessman/Entrepreneur/Actor

Frenchy is not his real name, but everyone knows him as Frenchy. I have known him for about twelve years—wow! Has it been twelve years already?—and his big heart and big energy are what anyone would want in a friend. Everyone knows Frenchy, and Frenchy knows everyone; he is always there with a hug and a smile. He is the "big idea" guy who, on more than one occasion, has helped me think through inspirations I've had and gave me things to think about that I would have never come up with. He is just so gosh darn adorable, like a big teddy bear, who I love and whose friendship I am lucky to have.

Frenchy owes his love of cooking to his mom. Besides teaching him the wonderful basics of cooking, she is a shining star in his life.

"My mother and father split up when I was about four years old. While she was single, she put herself through night school and got her master's in accounting. She eventually became a controller for a few different big companies and now owns her own accounting business, running it for coming up on twenty years now."

Her lifestyle taught Frenchy to be proud of who he is.

"She came out of the closet in the late 80s in a wealthy conservative town. I call her powerful because, at the time, that lifestyle was not very well-liked. She didn't care; she walked to the beat of her own drum. She is also a mountaineer, a river rafter, and an all-around outdoorsy badass. She is very open and spiritual, intelligent, and loving. She made me the man I am today as Dad wasn't around all that much."

I have had the pleasure of meeting Frenchy's mom a few times, and everything he says is true.

"The dish that was always the dish for me, and I know this is going to sound weird, is scrambled eggs. My mom has the magic touch when it comes to scrambled eggs." Scrambled eggs have become a part of his adult life. And upon taking inspiration from his mom, he has now perfected his own recipe which he makes every week. "From early childhood, that was the thing my mom made, and she made them really well."

Eggs need love. If you give them love, they will reward you with a perfect and delicious dish. "Cooking them at the right temperature with the right amount of butter, using very good butter, and how to dress it. Sometimes it's just salt and pepper, it's that simple, and sometimes it's melting some cheese in there."

It was an everyday staple for Frenchy growing up. Scrambled eggs and an English muffin. He usually had a tasty side to accompany it, but the real star of the plate was the scrambled eggs.

One of the most important things she taught him about cooking was understanding your heat and what that does to the food, depending on the type of food. Frenchy learned about controlling your cooking with heat when he was a teenager.

"I remember her explaining to me that by constantly moving the eggs at a low heat over and over again with cream and a whole lot of fluffing, prevented any of it from getting burned on the pan too long and drying out. And that made a lot of sense to me." Lessons to last a lifetime.

The idea of properly using heat for cooking is simple, but so many are unaware of its importance. Heat kills potential bacteria in raw food. However, if there is too much heat too quickly, it can burn or ruin the dish. It's how you use heat that can make or break a dish. I know many people who turn the heat up so that food will cook faster. When that happens, and food heats up too quickly, all the needed moisture goes out, and it is left dry. Yuck! When food is brought to temperature slowly, such as eggs, they retain the moisture giving you the perfect texture and flavor. The lesson here is that patience is definitely an important part of cooking. Frenchy's mom knew that.

Before he attained this knowledge, he simply enjoyed eating her eggs. As he got older, he understood why. Getting them to the right amount of fluff and beating them the right amount of time is important. Her eggs were simple and perfect, "they were delicious because of the fluffiness, because of the consistency, because she knew how to cook with heat." These lessons based on the fine art of properly cooking eggs have lasted a lifetime.

"Eggs are a perfect dish. People love to burn them, crisp them, making them not so great, in my opinion. Some people make them too runny, and some people know how to get them just right."

While the technical aspects of cooking eggs were an important lesson from his mom, it's the sense of comfort from that time spent in the kitchen with her that really makes this the one dish that brings him back to his childhood. That sense of warmth is what made the love of cooking and the details of how to perfect a dish stick with him for life.

"Now I've actually created what is my favorite scrambled egg dish," which is the recipe Frenchy will be sharing. "Everyone I've fed these eggs to have said these are the best eggs they've ever had in their life. I've learned from the best, my mother."

He took her lessons and created his own way of cooking, or as Frenchy says, "More like my whole ideology for cooking. I did take her recipe for cooking eggs and used it for how I prepare my eggs most of the time. Her recipe taught me the importance of heat. Most recipes call for a certain level of temperature with perhaps a temp change or two. Once I realized you could change it to whatever you wanted, I used that ideology to shape how I cook."

Now that he is an adult, he understands what an excellent source of protein eggs are. "I feel that eggs were God's gift to humans. Chickens are the perfect food. Not only are they good and high in protein themselves, but they also make eggs."

Eggs are healthy, and they come in their own perfect package. According to a 2020 WebMD article entitled "Health Benefits of Eggs," just one egg has six grams of protein with the white containing over half, four grams, of that protein. Eggs also contain all nine essential amino acids and have more nutrients per calorie than most other foods. I guess Frenchy is right.

Frenchy has had hundreds of scrambled eggs, and to this day, when he sees his mom and she asks him what he wants for breakfast, what do you think the answer is? Yep, scrambled eggs — every time. They are that good. Nostalgia only adds to the experience. Frenchy had many meals growing up as a kid, but none stood out like eggs. "There was nothing else that I felt stuck with me that was as special, that felt like a tradition. Mom's scrambled eggs; it doesn't get better than that."

"If you are going to do anything right, take your time," which not only applies to cooking the perfect eggs but pretty much everything else, too. Frenchy's life advice that makes perfect sense.

Here is how to make Frenchy's version of perfect scrambled eggs. Using the heat lessons taught to him by his mom. Frenchy adds feta cheese and garlic to his. If you are not a fan of either, use your imagination and add or substitute your favorite ingredients. This is all about the method.

FRENCHY'S SCRAMBLED EGGS INSPIRED BY MOM

INGREDIENTS:
- 1 ½ tablespoons butter (Frenchy uses Kerrygold butter which is an Irish butter, use if possible)
- 3 farm-fresh, cage-free eggs (if possible)
- 1 tablespoon half and half
- 1/2 - 1 teaspoon fresh garlic, finely minced
- feta cheese, quantity to your taste

DIRECTIONS:
1. Melt the butter in a pan on low heat, so the butter melts but does not brown.
2. In a bowl, whip (use a fork or whisk) the eggs very well with the half and half.

3. With the heat on low to medium-low, add the eggs to your pan. Patience is key.
4. Let the eggs just sit in the pan untouched, like you are going to make an omelet, for about 1 – 1 ½ minutes only. Watch to see that the eggs have started cooking; it doesn't take long.
5. Spread the feta and the garlic on the eggs while they are still raw on top.
6. Take your spatula and mix it up, turning it until it's cooked over, and keep cutting it until it gets fluffier. All the flavor will get absorbed into the eggs.
7. Transfer to a plate just before they are thoroughly cooked. If you finish cooking the eggs in the pan, they will get overdone. Let the heat finish cooking them there. You won't be disappointed.
8. Once your eggs are perfectly done, you can dress them any way you want. Frenchy likes to put his eggs over a bed of spinach with a little bit of salt, pepper, and maybe habanero chili. Or make breakfast tacos with some really good bacon.
9. Enjoy!

KAREN'S STORY

"People want honest, flavorful food, not some show-off meal that takes days to prepare."

—TED ALLEN

KAREN KRUSE—THE STORY OF RIVELS AND THE INSPI-RATION TO BECOME A CHEF

Age: 59 — Grandma/YouTube Creator

Karen's skills and talents as a chef are displayed on her You-Tube channel, *In the Kitchen with Karen.* She shares quick and easy recipes and attempts to use ten ingredients or less. Most recipes take under thirty minutes to prepare, and they are fabulous.

"My goal is to make recipes that are easy to make and taste great. I love to share my forty years of experience. I attended culinary school in San Diego, as well as Napa Valley, and became a personal chef as well as a caterer. I am happiest when I am in the kitchen."

Karen has the same passion for cooking that I do, and I love that. You can see it in everything she makes.

She was born in Akron, Ohio, and spent most of her young summers with her family visiting her Grandma Irene and Grandpa Ralph on their farm until her grandparents moved away when she was ten.

We see many fond memories going back to grandparents. The love you receive from a grandparent when you're a child is something to cherish if you were lucky enough to have a special relationship. Karen's story reflects that love and is directly connected to her passion for cooking today and her career as a chef.

Her story takes place on that farm.

"My grandparents had a big farm. It was about two or three acres and was absolutely beautiful with a waterfall in the back. They grew lots of vegetables—any vegetable you can think of. They had a giant farmhouse and a big basement with a root cellar. They did all kinds of canning with tons of shelves down there with every kind of canned vegetables and fruits you can think of. It was really, really neat!"

Root cellars have been used since at least the eighteenth century. According to *Rootwell Products*' 2016 article, "Everything you need to know about an Amazing Root Cellar," they are an underground structure used for the storage of vegetables, fruits, nuts, and other foods through the cold months. It was also an excellent place to store beer and wine. Since these rooms were underground, they kept food supplies at controlled temperature and steady humidity depending on what was being stored. Food could be stored without refrigeration. The name comes from the storage of root vegetables.

"I have memories of riding in the tractor with my grandpa and riding in this wagon that he used to tote all his supplies in." Yet, even better than riding in the wagon, is going to the basement.

Ralph owned a vending machine business. He had around fifty machines, and there was always one in his shop that needed to be worked on. "The best part is that he had candy vending machines. In the basement, he had shelves and shelves of every candy bar you can think of. We got to go down there and pick out any candy bars we wanted whenever we visited ... It was a kid's dream." Talk about luck; Karen was literally a kid in a candy store!

"My grandma was a really good cook. She had this red step stool; by the time I was three or four, I would always stand on it next to her at the stove and watch her cook." Can you see the makings of a future Chef here? "That's where I got my love of cooking from... she showed me all kinds of things to make and taught me how to cook."

I asked if her grandma was the inspiration in becoming a Chef, and Karen smiled and said, "Yes!" There you have it, childhood experiences leading to who we are as adults today.

Karen's childhood food memory is something unique that her grandma made at least once a week, German potato soup with rivels. Rivels translates to "lumps" and are tiny dumplings of sorts that are added to a soup, much like chicken and dumplings. Her grandparents were of German descent, and this dish is very common in that cuisine.

"My grandma taught me how to make it. It's a pretty simple soup with only six or seven ingredients." It's easy to see here why she favorites dishes with ten or fewer ingredients.

With it being grandpa's favorite, a simple dish to assemble, especially on busy work days, and made often. This hearty soup was a crowd-pleaser.

"I think it was a great meal for my grandpa because he could get so wrapped up in his projects for his vending machine business that it could just sit on the stove for quite a while until he finally came up. Usually after my Grandma had to tell him like four times that dinner was ready," Karen laughed. "She would often send us kids over there as messengers."

"I remember first tasting it when I was about six. Then when we got a bit older, around thirteen, my parents let me and my sister fly by ourselves back to Ohio in the summers for two weeks, and we would always ask her to make this soup. My sister and I would fight over who got more of the Rivels in their bowl. Those were the best part! And whenever I eat ANY kind of potato soup, it always reminds me of my grandma."

Karen's grandma would sometimes get creative with the soup, embellishing it with even more flavor. "She used to fry up bacon and crumble it on the top along with some green onion. She said you have to put lots and lots of pepper in your soup, so we always had lots of pepper." Karen chuckled, relaying this part of her memory.

"I still make it today. It reminds me most of my grandparents since that was one of their favorite dishes. It was just a nice comfort food dish ... It reminds me of my childhood." Comfort is love and security, and that is what Karen found in this glorious soup. It's like a warm blanket in soup form.

The beautiful farm has since been sold. Nevertheless, the memories live on in Karen's heart and the soup in Karen's kitchen. And hopefully, it will soon be in yours.

GRANDMA IRENE'S GERMAN POTATO SOUP WITH RIVELS

INGREDIENTS:
- 6–7 medium potatoes (Karen likes Yukon Gold), diced
- 1/2 cup finely diced sweet yellow onion
- 1/2 cup finely diced celery
- 2 tablespoons butter
- 2 cups chicken stock
- 1 12oz can evaporated Milk
- 1/2 teaspoon salt
- 1/2 teaspoon pepper

FOR THE RIVELS:
- 1 large egg, beaten
- 1/2 cup all-purpose flour

- 1/4 teaspoon salt

DIRECTIONS:

1. In a dutch oven or soup pot over medium heat, melt the 2 Tablespoons of butter, add the celery and the onion.
2. Sauté over medium heat until translucent. This should take about 5 minutes.
3. Then add in your diced Potatoes and your Chicken stock.
4. Cover the pot and simmer on medium-low for 20 minutes or until the potatoes are fork-tender.
5. In a separate bowl, beat your egg and slowly incorporate the flour and salt until a soft dough forms.
6. Add the evaporated milk to the soup and simmer for 5 minutes.
7. Then, pinch off small pieces of the dough from the bowl and drop them into the soup.
8. Put the lid on and simmer for another 5 minutes.
9. Add more salt and pepper if needed.
10. Enjoy!

ILANA'S STORY

"To me, food is as much about the moment, the occasion, the location and the company as it is about the taste."

—HESTON BLUMENTHAL

IILANA PARSONS—THE STORY OF PEPPERS, ONIONS, AND BRUNCH

Age: 55 — Sister/Friend/Navy Wife

It's fun to travel back in time. Ilana and I were Sigma Kappa sorority sisters in college. It was great seeing each other again and talking about "the good old days," although these are pretty good days as well. This interview brought me back to our parties, fundraisers, laughter, and crazy antics. Ilana hasn't changed one bit. It's always so insightful to hear childhood stories about someone to get a better understanding of who they are. For me, to learn about their one dish that brings them back to their childhood is so intriguing. I never know what someone is going to say when I ask them this question. Ilana did not disappoint.

Ilana's childhood memory is not exactly a dish; instead, it's an integral part of many dishes she ate growing up. She told me, "This recipe is a base for basically whatever you want."

Her mom, Gloria, was the daughter of Sicilian parents. They emigrated to New York, where they met, eloped, and started a family. She prized her family culinary traditions, which have also now carried into Ilana's home. It's a simple combination of peppers and onions.

"I make them when we host brunch. I serve them on their own, add them to eggs, put them on a bagel, whatever." The options are endless.

This is the base for the Italian classic, sausage and peppers, which was a staple in Ilana's house when she was growing up. "The base works beautifully no matter what protein you use."

"My parents were older. My dad, Marcus, fought in World War II, and my mom was an Arthur Murray dancer in the 1940s."

According to the history section of the Arthur Murray website, Arthur Murray started the Arthur Murray Dance Studios in the 1930s with the slogan, "If you can walk, we can teach you how to dance." That was ninety years ago. Today, there are 270 Arthur Murray dance studios in twenty-two countries. Gloria worked with Arthur Murray himself and his wife Kathryn, where she helped create the manual for instructors in addition to teaching. Wow!

"In addition to her studio work during this time, mom also worked at resorts as an instructor. Summers meant New England, and winters took her to Florida, the Bahamas, and Cuba. She used the name Gloria Carlton while dancing. Much like movie studios renamed actors, Arthur Murray renamed his instructors."

Ilana took me back to WWII and told me the story of her mom right before the US entered the war. On December 7, 1941, Pearl Harbor was attacked and brought the United States into World War II. Gloria was getting ready for a date at the time; her memories were so clear. According to what Gloria shared with Ilana, "There was a radio on top of the fridge, and when the news broke, she started sobbing because she knew we were going to go to war. She knew this would force us to join the war, and all the men in the family, the neighborhood, the country would soon be shipping out, and the world would never be the same."

It wouldn't be until twenty years post-war that Ilana's parents met and subsequently married.

Marcus graduated from UCLA in 1940 and was an accountant at the time in Los Angeles. Sadly, his career path was put on hold on that fateful day in 1941.

"Following the attack on Pearl Harbor, he and his brother, Uncle Augie, enlisted like so many of their peers. Dad served in the Army Air Corps, pre-Air Force, in Europe. He was a sergeant, financial technician/payroll clerk who served from 1942-45. Uncle Augie, William Kalb, was a scout in the U.S. Marine Corps who served in the Pacific. Following the war, he returned to UCLA to complete his law studies. Both dad and Augie practiced law in Los Angeles and met for lunch weekly into the 1980s."

As Ilana's parents were older, she grew up in a house where scratch cooking was a daily occurrence. Scratch cooking was the order of the day in the 1940s, making unassuming ingredients work for many different dishes. There were convenience foods around, but it was common to make everything yourself and make multiple weekly trips to the market, hence her childhood dish.

"My mom was the one that went to the market a couple of times every week. I still don't understand how to plan meals for a whole week." Ilana, like her mom, plans meals as the week progresses.

To this day, Ilana mainly cooks from scratch. Today there are endless varieties of quick, easy-to-prepare meals, but Ilana still prefers to cook old school. I have to agree; I also tend to cook from scratch every night—perhaps since my focus is cooking from the past. For instance, I never buy prepared salad dressing. I make it fresh every time for that one special salad. The more time I can spend in the kitchen, the better. It's truly my Zen space. When we have positive childhood experiences with food, we tend to emulate them later in life — which is exactly what Ilana does today.

"Mom never followed recipes. My learning to cook was based on observation and improvisation. Over the years, mom would experiment and change how she prepared meals. I make adjustments based on my personal preferences."

Ilana's Italian family lived in Studio City, California, in a big Jewish community. On Christmas Day, all her friends who didn't celebrate the holiday would come over to the house. They were the house that everyone would come over to for brunch. "My parents were famous for brunch. They hosted parties year-round."

"I was the child that learned how to make a really good Old Fashioned by the third grade since my parents would always have their friends over. They were of the cocktail generation."

She can still make a really good Old Fashioned. Her early "bartending" skills led her to the path she is on now, managing a coffee store.

Peppers and onions were always in attendance at brunch. Though, this dish isn't just for that meal; it's for breakfast, lunch, and dinner as well. Brunch was a big thing in Ilana's house, and that is why she loves it today.

"The thing with peppers and onions is it was used in a bunch of different meals. When it came to brunch, my dad was the king of eggs. It was his one activity." He was a busy attorney and certified public accountant; however, the one time he got into the kitchen was to make himself eggs. He used to cook peppers and onions mixed in with his eggs. Ilana prefers hers on the side.

These two ingredients made an appearance on the table every other week. Every other week through your childhood, there are many peppers and onions, with some protein. Sausage and peppers were common.

"And always with crusty bread. My grandfather, Benjamin Kalb, was a baker who emigrated from Austria, so my parents were bread snobs."

Ilana still makes her staple to this day, usually once a month. She loves them with steak or sausage. It's those happy childhood memories that make you want to relive them as an adult. Your amygdala decided it liked the experience, and your hippocampus brings you right back. We are a product of our upbringing, and a house full of family, friends, and good food is such a marvelous thing to want to continue as an adult.

"Once you have the peppers and onions, you can then figure out what you have in the house' and build from there. You can do anything with it."

Ilana is passionate about her peppers and onions, and I can't wait to try it with a bagel and cream cheese.

ILANA'S FAMILY'S PEPPERS AND ONIONS

There are no specific quantities for this dish. It depends on the amount you would like to make. Use as many green, yellow, red, or orange bell peppers and onions as you like. For two people, Ilana suggests three peppers and one onion. Tip: keep in mind that peppers cook down quite a bit, so you will always yield about half of what you have raw.

INGREDIENTS:

- green, red, yellow and/or orange peppers, sliced thin
- 1 yellow onion (or more if you prefer), sliced thin
- 1 tablespoon butter
- 1 tablespoon olive oil
- Salt and pepper to taste
- Protein of your choice - optional (protein quantity depends on personal preference)

DIRECTIONS:

1. Cook the peppers and onions in a large lidded pan with butter and olive oil, about 1 tablespoon of each, over medium heat.
2. Once the peppers and onions are cooked down, set them aside to rest, lid on, no heat, and start any protein if you like.
3. While the protein is cooking, raise the heat on the peppers and onions to caramelize.
4. Once they start to turn golden, they are done. Add salt and pepper to taste.
5. They are great on their own.
6. Enjoy!

If you too would like to enjoy these with a steak, Ilana suggests adding salt and lots of freshly ground pepper and searing the steak in a cast-iron pan over high heat with a little butter. Cook steak to preferred doneness and plate immediately. Pile the peppers and onions over the steak and enjoy, always with crusty bread and wine.

ALEXIS' STORY

"A recipe has no soul. You, as the cook, must bring soul to the recipe."

—THOMAS KELLER

CHEF ALEXIS HERNANDEZ–THE STORY OF CUBAN BEANS AND RICE AND THE UNEXPECTED ROAD TO CULINARY SCHOOL

Age 51, Chef

If you enjoy cooking competitions, you may have seen Alexis Hernandez on your television. He has competed in *The Next Food Network Star* (Season 6), *Cutthroat Kitchen* (Crabs of Steel), *Cutthroat Kitchen Evilicious* (20,000 Leagues Under the Prep Table), and has appeared on CNN's *Sabores*. On Cutthroat Kitchen, he portrayed the cocky and arrogant villain, but that was only his persona for the show; he is just a sweetheart with the kindest personality in real life.

"When the cameras were on, I had to maintain the evil persona, the evil Alexis. I would get the worst comments on Twitter, and I was like 'Oh my God, it's a show!'" Always take what you see on TV with a grain of salt.

Alexis is a classically trained chef. He is now sharing his cooking skills on YouTube on his channel, *The Other Side of the Stove*. "I have successfully owned my own restaurant and catering business. Today the view from my stove has changed. Gathering all the choice experiences from my journey, I want to take you to the other side of the stove. Here, the stove looks different now for me."

Alexis is an American-born Cuban, and this cultural background has given him many engaging stories. His parents, Adalberto and Graciela, immigrated to the United States from Cuba in 1965 "before Castro showed his colors," and people were free to leave. His father was a Baptist minister, and the family moved to New York so he could pursue his calling to religious work further. Alexis grew up in Union City, New Jersey, in the parsonage at his father's church.

"I grew up in a very Italian neighborhood early on, then it turned very Latino from many countries." He had neighbors from Puerto Rico, Columbia, El Salvador, and many other Latin countries. English is his second language. "When I went to school, there were people that looked like me, to varying degrees. We all spoke English, but Spanish was our first language."

Adalberto was the main cook in the family. "He liked cooking and enjoyed it, and it was pleasurable for him to experiment in the kitchen. He loved entertaining people and was very outgoing; he was not a wallflower. My mother was less social than my dad, however did cook when my father was not able to cook because he was at work."

I asked Alexis what his childhood food memory was. "I know this sounds like such a stereotype, but I love my black beans and rice. I used to not like it, meaning it was too ethnic."

It was something that the family ate every day when he was growing up.

"Dinner was always some type of white rice, beans, and a meat. Sometimes my mother would get iceberg lettuce," which was very common in the 1970s before we had the varieties we have now, "and put vinegar on it, which was so gross. We would eat it all the time."

"We're having black beans again?" he would say to his mom. His mom would say, "You're ungrateful, some people don't have food!" And Alexis would say, "I don't want it, leave me alone!" I would wager to bet that this exchange was had in many other homes.

If Alexis didn't like black beans and rice, how did it wind up becoming the one dish that brings him back to his childhood, his comfort food?

"When you're eating something every week or almost every day, you kind of don't really want to eat it anymore. When

I went to seminary college, you would not see me trying to make beans in the dorm ... I was trying to make pasta, make Greek meatballs, anything that wasn't Cuban food. I would try and learn to cook from magazines or books. Black beans becoming my comfort food was a gradual journey as I grew older. I was around thirty-five when I went to Asia de Cuba, a restaurant in New York, and had creamy congri, and I thought ... Was this what I was eating growing up? It was delicious! I thought, 'Why am I avoiding it and choosing other cuisines instead of the food I grew up eating?'"

Alexis' parents would make one pot of black beans to last the week. Every day, his mom took some beans for dinner. As the week progressed, the beans would get eaten, and the cooking liquid would remain in the pot.

"Towards the end of the week, the beans were gone, and all that was left was the cooking water. She would use the cooking liquid to make that night's rice so it would come out dark." This is what Alexis calls Congri. Blackish rice with just a few beans that remained. "When you got congri, you knew it was the end of the week."

"Church was every day of my life. I started to follow in my father's footsteps by going to seminary college, but the gay thing kind of shot it down. The world wasn't ready. I said, 'God, you are going to have to love me because it's not going away.'" Especially during this time period, being gay did not seem compatible with his desire to become a minister.

"I realized that these feelings weren't changing. When I was in my teens, I thought, 'When I'm eighteen, this will resolve itself,' but it did not. When I graduated from seminary, I was in my early twenties, and my gay feelings had not gone away. Ultimately I decided while attending seminary that there was no opportunity at that time for me to be an openly gay minister. The world wasn't ready for it, and my own world wasn't ready for it." Even with this dilemma, Alexis did complete seminary.

After seminary, he went on a path of self-discovery, which eventually led him to culinary school. "I had no interest in going to culinary school, nor did I think about it at the time." However, while in seminary, he discovered a whole new world of food. "I was eating things I've never heard of like a club sandwich, a chef's salads, and I was like, what's a meatloaf?"

Meatloaf was something Alexis was delighted to discover. "For me to see the cube of meat, the meatloaf, with mashed potatoes ... it was not a thing I ate growing up. And the gravy, I asked 'What's that brown stuff?' and was told, it's gravy. The kids in seminary would look at the meatloaf and say, 'Ewe, you're going to eat that?' and I said, 'Why? It's so delicious.'" Alexis thought back to how often he was served beans and rice growing up and becoming tired of it. He realized this is the exact same way his new friends thought about meatloaf, but it was new to him and delightful. "When I got older, I thought, 'Oh, meatloaf was their version of my black beans and rice.'"

"At the time that the culinary school thing came about, I had moved to our farm in Indiana." Marty, Alexis' husband, convinced him to think about culinary school. "He said that it would be great for me and that now I would know how to do the things in the kitchen that I saw at restaurants."

Marty actually applied to culinary school, The National Center for Hospitality studies, for Alexis. The surprise was receiving his letter of acceptance and his chef whites (coat) in the mail. He was accepted before he even knew about it. Marty knew Alexis well and clearly loved him very much. Alexis was dedicated, so much so that he went on to complete his two-year culinary program in one year.

As a chef, he went on to follow his passion by owning and operating his own restaurant. All his years of self-discovery, and with the influence of his husband, lead him to the success he is today. It all started with very humble beginnings of black beans and rice.

Today as an adult, Alexis eats black beans almost every day. Although his beans and rice now have a very "chefy" influence.

"I'll make salmon and black beans or black beans with rice infused with rosemary. I'll do black beans with cardamom. Sometimes it's red beans, and sometimes it's no rice. When I'm lazy, I'll open a can of black beans, and I know some people make fun of me, but it's fine. You think after being at work as a chef all day, sometimes fourteen hours, I'm going to come home and make sure that I soaked the beans? No! Canned! I'm going to sauté some onions first, get the aromatics going, some garlic, and oregano, then I'm going to dump the can of beans in, mix it around, bring it to a boil and that's it."

Aromatics are vegetables that have a deep rounded flavor and aroma when crushed, such as garlic, fresh herbs, ginger, chili peppers, onions, carrots, and many other similar ingredients.

"It's comforting to me, and I love it. It gives me this happiness that I can't explain when I eat it." We all have our stories and Alexis finding comfort in a can of jazzed-up black beans takes him right home to his house with his parents. With that, Alexis has shared his dad's recipe for black beans and rice, which he translated from Spanish for us. Thank you, Alexis.

ADALBERTO'S FAVORITE BLACK BEANS

"This is translated from my father's original handwritten black bean recipe that he brought from Cuba. I enjoyed this recipe throughout my young adulthood almost every day."

INGREDIENTS:
- 1 pound of dry black beans
- 2 tablespoons of oil
- 1 medium onion, chopped
- Half a green bell pepper, chopped
- 2 cloves of garlic, crushed
- 1 tablespoon of dried oregano
- 1/8 teaspoon of dried cumin
- 2 tablespoons of dry white wine
- Salt to taste
- 1/4 teaspoon of black pepper
- 1 bay leaf

- 1 packet of Sazon like Goya (without color — no red annatto (This is a Puerto Rican spice that can be found online or in Hispanic markets)

DIRECTIONS:

1. Go through the beans removing any broken pieces or debris that you may find.
2. Put the beans in a pot, fill with water (about 10 cups of water) and soak for about 3 to 4 hours, but letting the beans soak overnight is best.
3. Keeping the water, move the pot of beans to the stove, bring to a boil on high heat.
4. While the beans are cooking, in a sauté pan, combine the oil, garlic, onion, peppers, oregano, cumin, and bay leaf. On medium heat, mix and cook ingredients down. (you are making what is known as a sofrito)
5. Go back to your beans, lower the heat to a simmer for about an hour or until all the beans have softened.
6. Once the beans are done, add the dry white wine, stir, then add the sofrito.
7. Lastly, add the black pepper and the Sazon seasoning packet into the beans and stir.
8. Enjoy!

FOR THE RICE:

"My father would use a 1:1 ratio with regular long-grain rice. He would wash the rice 3–4 times to remove the starch. If he used a cup of washed rice, he would use a cup of water, a little salt, and oil. Then cook it on the stove. First, bring to a boil, then reduce heat and cover for about 20–25 minutes until water is fully absorbed."

SHARLA'S STORY

"Life is uncertain. Eat dessert first."

—ERNESTINE ULMER

SHARLA HULSEY—THE STORY OF ALL THINGS STRAW-BERRY

52, Pastor/Lover of all things Food and Drink

Sharla is one of my 14k+ viewers and a fellow foodie. Before I had the pleasure of meeting her for this book, I only knew her from her fun childhood memories which she shared on my channel. Reading these memories is such a gift. I am grateful to Sharla for taking the time to be part of this book. Sharla, say hello to your beautiful cat, Archie, who often walked across the screen during the interview.

I began this interview the same way I had with every single one of them: by asking, "What is the one dish that brings you back to your childhood?" Sharla started, "It has been really hard to think of just one because pretty much my whole life and all my memories revolved around food. My dad ran a restaurant when I was growing up, my grandpa had a grocery store, his mother had a restaurant, my great-grandpa on my mom's side had a butcher shop, and I have a cousin that is a chef." Sharla wasn't kidding. Her whole life revolved around food; her whole family was in the food business in one way or another.

This is absolutely a food family, and I am extremely jealous. "We talk about food all the time." Her church folks tease her; if they go on vacation to a location that she has also visited, when they return, Sharla asks, "Where did you go to eat?". The restaurants at the destination are what Sharla wants to talk about. I love that she remembers her vacations by the food she ate.

"What finally came to my mind as far as a food memory was strawberries."

You just never know what someone will say, and this just brought a big smile to my face. I wondered how strawberries became such a significant part of her life. It turns out there is some family history to this.

"My mom, Claudia, tells the story, and I don't remember this; this was before my time. She said that when she was growing up, when strawberries were in season, Gram Dorothy would go get a flat of strawberries. They would eat strawberries at every meal until they were gone, and then Gram would go get another one."

They would keep up the love of eating until strawberry season was over. Strawberry season, that was something special. Nowadays, it's always strawberry season — although they still seem to taste better in the summer, I think.

"When strawberry season was over, my mom didn't care if she ever saw another strawberry until the next year."

Sharla grew up in Coffeyville, Kansas, which is right on the state line of Kansas and Oklahoma. She told me that it was a small town that peaked in the 1950s at about seventeen thousand people; they are down to about ten thousand people now. It was a town built around four or five brick manufacturing plants. Coffeyville bricks, which was stamped right into each individual piece, were something to value. At Baker University in Baldwin City, Kansas, there is an entrance that's made up of Coffeyville bricks, which the class of 1928 put in.

"Gram made scratch biscuits for papa every morning from the day after they got married until the day she died. The day after was an important time. The first morning of their marriage, gram got up and made papa biscuits before he went to work, and after he ate his breakfast, on his way out the door, he said to his brand-new wife, 'Go over to my mom's house and have her teach you how to make biscuits.'" I literally said "Ouch!" during the interview. Apparently, she did, and they went on to enjoy a forty-seven-year marriage until she passed. Gram passed away young at sixty-five, and papa lived to be ninety-one.

Sharla learned how to make biscuits from her Gram when she was about ten or eleven and has been making them ever since.

"When I go to see my mom and dad, my dad always asks me if I'm going to make biscuits while I'm there." Her parents are well set and do not need anything, so her gifts to them are always making homemade biscuits. Homemade gifts are so heartfelt.

Sharla's love of all things strawberries came from her grandma. "The main thing I remember about gram and her strawberries was that case of "Empress" preserves in her metal pantry cabinet, and papa having his preserves on his biscuits."

"I do, of course, remember gram making biscuits." With biscuits comes strawberries. "Strawberries are just something that has been present all my life. We had shortcake at least once every summer. My mom made it in two big pieces instead of individual cut rounds like I do these days. She would bake them on a cookie sheet, and then when they came out of the oven, she would spread them with butter."

"Several times, we went up to a farm/market between Coffeyville and Independence and picked our own berries. She would mash them and put them in a Tupperware container. She collects vintage Tupperware, among lots of other things ..." Of course, what would the 1970s be without Tupperware?

The history behind strawberry shortcakes started with an unleavened cookie of sorts in Europe. A recipe for a rich cookie was published in a 1588 Elizabethan cookbook. This "cookie" was the predecessor to the scone. However, strawberry shortcake is all-American. As Chef Mireille relays in her 2016 article, "Strawberry Shortcake — a History Lesson and a Recipe," Americans discovered they could, with the advent of leavening agents — baking powder and baking soda — lighten up the dough and create light and fluffy biscuits. In 1847, creative cooks suggested layering these new fluffy biscuits with strawberries. And finally, in 1862, a magazine published in Rochester, New York, added cream to the equation. And just like that, the strawberry shortcake as we know it was born.

The article "Strawberries & More, History & Lore" by the *University of Illinois Extension* tells us that the strawberry is a member of the rose family and is the only fruit with seeds on the outside. It is a true symbol for Venus, the goddess of love, because of its heart shape and red color. Also, legend has it that if you break a double strawberry in half and share it with someone special, you will fall in love with each other. Is it true? That's the legend, at least. Oh, by the way, *National Today* notes that National Strawberry Day is June 14, which is the peak of strawberry season. Go celebrate!

Sharla's love for strawberries — merged with her childhood experiences — continue to influence her today. "As an adult, I started doing what Gram did by stopping at a stand on my way home from work and buying a flat of strawberries, making shortcake and jam and freezing some of them, then getting another flat over and over till strawberry season was over."

Strawberry shortcake means childhood to Sharla. Here is the recipe for her grandma's famous biscuits, made daily for her grandpa, that she learned how to make on day two of her marriage. She gives options below for both biscuits and shortcake.

GRAM'S BAKING POWDER BISCUITS AND STRAWBERRY SHORTCAKE

SHORTCAKE INGREDIENTS:
- 2 cups all-purpose flour
- 3 rounded teaspoons baking powder
- 1 teaspoon sugar (optional)
- ¾ teaspoon salt
- 1/3 cup shortening (for biscuits) or 1/2 cup butter (for shortcake)
- ½ cup milk

STRAWBERRY FILLING INGREDIENTS:
- 1 pint-sized basket of strawberries (or more if you really love them)
- sugar, about 2 tablespoons sugar to every basket (pint) of strawberries. The sweetness of berries isn't always consistent; taste your berries first
- whipped cream, as much as you love
- ice cream, optional

DIRECTIONS:
1. In a bowl, mix dry ingredients for the shortcake/biscuit and cut in shortening with fork, pastry blender, or fingers.

2. Stir in milk <u>slowly</u> until a "shaggy" dough forms into a ball (It's lumpy yet well-mixed, with no dry spots of flour, to make a rough-looking dough. If it's got enough liquid to form into a ball, it's probably too wet.)

3. Place the dough onto a floured surface and pat out about ¾" thick.

4. Cut the dough with a biscuit cutter, clean can, or glass cup — whatever you've got; it's a Depression recipe.

5. Place dough rounds in a cast-iron skillet or a baking pan about 2" deep so that biscuits are touching, no need to grease either pan

6. Bake at 400F to 425F for 10-12 minutes, until tops are golden and biscuits are firm to the touch.

7. If making shortcake, brush with melted butter after baking.

8. Put clean, sliced (or whole if they're small) strawberries in a bowl and mix with sugar to taste.

9. Let sit for a while to macerate (soften), then use a potato masher to smash some of the berries, while leaving some whole. Serve on shortcake and top with whipped cream and/or ice cream.

10. Enjoy!

MIKE'S STORY

"If God had intended us to follow recipes, he wouldn't have given us grandmothers."

—LINDA HENLEY

MIKE WOLFORD—THE STORY OF GRANDMA HELEN'S BIG YELLOW POT
Age 53, YouTube Creator

Mike is a passionate outdoor cook and is affectionately known as "El Duderino." Mike's channel, *The Dudes Kitchen n Grill*, is all about cooking delicious things outdoors. The first time I saw Mike's show, I smiled. Here was a very laidback guy drinking a White Russian in his backyard and grilling something yummy. I don't remember the exact dish he was making, but I knew I wanted to eat it. "My goal is to show you that anyone can make meals outside and have fun at the same time. We're the channel for slackers who like to cook. So, grab a White Russian, and let's do this." Mike is always celebrating and drinking his favorite cocktail, although he's rarely met a beer he hasn't liked.

His story takes place in the very early 1970s, beginning when he was around four years old. The world for a young boy at that time was far from the chill life he loves today. America was at war. "I remember watching TV at home in the Tri-cities, Washington, and watching the news showing helicopters with troops jumping out during the Vietnam War. This is the only reason I remember the time frame." It carried a tremendous impact for someone so young, so much so that Mike has remembered it throughout his entire life.

Despite having such somber memories of watching the war on TV, Mike recalls much of his childhood fondly. He loved visiting his grandparents, and he would spend most of his summers and Christmas breaks with them. His grandfather, Joe, was a dairyman and had a cattle ranch in Prosser, Washington. He had horses, cows, and two corrals. Why two? Mike didn't know. But what he did know was that he grew a garden in one of the corrals. This garden was huge and full of potatoes, corn, peas, and all sorts of remarkable produce.

Over by the corral, there was a huge haystack, and right by the haystack, his grandfather dug a huge hole. What was this for? To keep the potatoes, and anything else they harvested, safe for the fall and winter. He would then cover this "underground produce storage" with the hay.

Mike's grandmother, Helen, also had a garden, and this was located right over an old bomb shelter that his grandparents built in the early 1960s. In her garden, she grew radishes, rutabagas, tomatoes, and all sorts of lettuces. Since they lived on a cattle ranch, they would butcher a cow once a year. Between the cow and the two gardens, they pretty much had what they needed to eat all winter long.

Grandma Helen was in charge of cooking. Since Mike is such a passionate cook today, I asked him if he helped her cook, and the answer was, "No, grandma was the cook. I once saw grandpa cooking hamburgers, and it was a mess."

Farm cooking was fresh cooking. There was no microwave. Nothing was out of a box. Everything was made right in Helen's kitchen, and everything was simple. Going to the grocery store was rare. They would go from time to time to pick up odds and ends; however, the majority came from the farm. They would freeze their butter and milk and have gallons on hand. That is how they lived.

One of Mike's fondest memories of visiting his grandparents was going in the cupboard and picking out potatoes, corn, or one of the many vegetables available and bringing it to his grandmother in the kitchen. She would make dinner out of his selections.

Mike's biggest food memory is Grandma Helen's pot roast. "This was always cooked in the same yellow pot, and she always made this dish when I visited." Mike has fond memories of this cooking vessel. The dish was simply a big chuck roast with farm-fresh potatoes, carrots, and water. "It was simple and delicious. There was enough to last a few days." His grandparents were friends with a professional wrestler named "Lumberjack Luke." Luke got into the buffalo business. Since they were friends, his grandfather started buying buffalo from him. So, besides beef, the famous pot roast was sometimes made with buffalo.

This was her signature dish, and that is how he remembers his grandparents. His memories of this dish go from the early 1970s all the way through the late 1980s, tried and true. This dish defined who his grandparents were to him. "My grandparents were very simple, lived on a dairy farm that I loved, and being a child of a messy divorce, going there always brought comfort to me. The smells alone of walking around their place was the best feeling to me. My Grandfather loved roast beef, and Grandma made her roast the way he liked it, simple with tons of gravy, which she made using the water and fat from the roast, adding a little flour. The smell alone, for me, could brighten up the worst of days and make the best of days just that much better. I have never smelled or tasted anything quite like it again, but I do know this recipe is just about as close as I would ever get to being back at their place." It was contentment, and young Mike could always expect it.

It wouldn't be a visit to his grandparents without this memorable pot roast cooked in the old yellow pot—especially since he got to pick out the vegetables. To this day, every time he smells a roast, it brings back great memories. That is what food does. Sadly, that yellow pot no longer exists, but the recipe does and defines simplicity with some love mixed in. Try El Duderino's childhood memory, and if you have a yellow pot, all the better!

GRANDMA HELEN'S POT ROAST

This is the exact recipe Mike gave me from his memory. As you can see, you will need to estimate quantities based on your preference. I put my notes in the parenthesis.

INGREDIENTS:

- 1 large chuck roast (Mike didn't specify weight; usually it is ½ - ¾ lb. per person depending on appetite)
- 2 cups water
- carrots, peeled and sliced in large chunks (as much as you like)
- potatoes, peeled and diced in large pieces (as much as you like)
- 1 tablespoon cornstarch or flour

DIRECTIONS:

1. Place roast in a baking or roasting pan and sprinkle with salt and pepper to your taste.
2. Add two cups of water to the bottom.
3. Cover and cook at 350F until the internal temperature reaches 150-160 degrees. (This should take 2-3 hours)
4. About halfway through cooking, add as many carrots and potatoes as you like to the pot.
5. Once roast is ready, remove from the oven. Keep it in the pan covered, and let rest (about 10–20 minutes).
6. Pour the drippings from the roast into a saucepan.
7. Place saucepan over medium heat and add (about 1 TBS) cornstarch or flour to the pan and stir until it thickens. (Start with 1 TBS and continue to add more until you reach your desired thickness,) Stir continually until you have smooth and slightly thickened gravy.

8. Slice roast and add gravy along with salt and pepper to taste.
9. Serve with carrots and potatoes
10. Enjoy!

BRET'S STORY

———

"People will travel anywhere for good food, it's crazy."

—RENE REDZEPI

BRET BERLIN—THE STORY OF A LOVE LANGUAGE, TRAVEL, AND A JEWISH GRANDMA'S SPECIALTY

Age 53, Dad/Food Enthusiast

Cooking, and later, traveling, has been a major part of Bret's life for as long as he can remember. At the time of this book's writing, Bret's marital status is single. In my opinion, he's is quite the catch. Okay, he is a good friend of mine, but I think that makes my opinion stronger.

At the time of this interview, Bret has been doing quite a bit of thinking about what he wants in a partner, what kind of life he wants to build and what his love language might be.

According to Gary Chapman, author of *5 Love Languages*, there are five "languages" to describe how we want to feel love from a partner. These include words of affirmation, acts of service, receiving gifts, quality time, and physical touch. Everyone has different love languages that resonate with them. Mine happens to be a romantic evening out. Bret adapted this concept to better suit him and determined his own love language—food. According to Bret, a love language can be anything that resonates with you, what you give to show love and receive love, so food it is! Food is not part of the *5 Love Languages* in Chapman's book; this is simply Bret's loving creation. When he cares about someone, he makes them a meal. This is Bret's way of sharing his heart and showing love. Over a meal, he can offer support, love, advice, or just an ear to listen, and he loves to cook for people.

Through cooking and food, Bret expresses himself and his sense of community. "Thinking back in time, most of the important milestones in my life have happened around the dinner table." Whether he's making meals for people or they're all in the kitchen cooking together. The loving experience of sharing a meal with friends or family is universal.

His first realization of his true love for cooking came when he was growing up in the 1970s with his mom. Bret was in elementary school at the time, in the fourth or fifth grade. "During this decade, there was a very popular 1968 book series that found a place in many American homes called "Time-Life Foods of the World." Time-Life came out with many different book series during this period, and this particular gem was a twenty-four-book series which, once ordered, the lucky recipient would receive a new set of two books every month. These were fabulous books, each highlighting a different country. Not only would there be recipes from each country, but stories about the country to go along with them. I know all of this because we had the same set in my home growing up. They were captivating.

This series is the base of his childhood memories and his love of cooking. Every month Bret and his mom would receive the set of two books, a hard-covered cookbook and a soft-covered spiral picture book highlighting one particular country. The books were interactive with each other. A particular picture in the spiral book showing people eating something delicious, such as curry from Thailand, would have a footnote saying something like, "If you would like to see the recipe for this dish, go to the cookbook on page XX." The reader would then open the accompanying book to find the recipe. "Every month represented a different region or country, and when it arrived, I thought about what it would be like to travel to Thailand or whatever country that month's book would happen to be."

Bret grew up in a highly rural part of North Florida, and he was in charge of cooking dinner for himself and his single mom. Yes, he was in elementary school at the time, but the rule was, whoever cooked, didn't have to clean up. Thus, he chose to cook! "There were no large grocery stores in my town, just a small store down the street with limited items."

Every day, when he got home from school, he went straight to his Time-Life books for inspiration. He picked a dish, made a shopping list, and went to the grocery store. "It was a creative outlet, a way to escape boredom and probably a way to procrastinate from doing homework. I just liked to cook." It was common for only about half of the ingredients he needed to be available; specialty items were just not available in his small town. "I would look at the picture and guess substitutions." Keep in mind, the internet was still far in the future, so there was no way to look things up.

Cooking dinner with half of the needed ingredients and half-guessed ones turned out to be a taste-as-you-go experience. "My goal was to make it taste good and to make it look like the picture in the book. I didn't know what it was supposed to taste like, but it usually came out great." The best part was that in his mind, he was able to travel the world and experience it through the book's pictures and food. His experience of finding the dish, going on his bike to the grocery store, figuring things out, cooking dinner, and not having to clean up was worth it.

In childhood, Bret traveled the world through cooking. Since then, he's been able to experience these different tastes through actual travel. He has traveled to Thailand, Chile, Spain, Scotland, Mexico, Germany, and Switzerland. "I learned some local cooking everywhere my travels took me."

His passion for cooking was inspired not only by his set of books but also by his grandma, Gigi. She also instilled Bret's curiosity for food and cooking.

Bret's grandma just turned 101. That in and of itself is quite an accomplishment. She's a beautiful true Jewish grandma on his mother's side. "It wasn't a dish from my books, but from tradition and heart." He is the eldest of fifteen grandkids.

Back when she was more mobile, all holidays and birthdays were celebrated at her house. "A combination of my grandmother's cooking and the Time-Life books ignited my curiosity for both food and travel. I connected with my grandma through the love of food. When Gigi was making dinner, she made at least ten different dishes, and they would come out to the table when they were ready. This was not a dinner when everything was at the table when you sat down. They would come out as they were ready. There were adult's tables and kid's tables all over her house. Who else had that growing up? Everyone just waited, and when the food came out, it was a free for all. If you waited, you would miss out."

Of all the dishes she made, her stuffed cabbage was his favorite. And that is Bret's dish that brings him back to his childhood.

Stuffed cabbage is a classic Jewish dish comprising of ground meat and rice mixed together and rolled up in softened cabbage leaves covered in a beautiful sweet and sour tomato sauce. When he was little, he would always miss out on the aforementioned free for all since he was small. But fear not, grandma was there with her finger motioning him to come into the kitchen where she had a special plate of her famous stuffed cabbage waiting for him. This lasted until his Bar Mitzvah — when a Jewish boy turns thirteen and, in the eyes of the religion, becomes a man. Now that he was a "man," she told him he was now old enough to fend for himself.

"My grandma did teach me how to cook some dishes. My interest in cooking was developed through both watching her in the kitchen making the dishes I grew up on and the Time-Life books I read." It was a combination of the two that made Bret who he is today. It is how he came to his self-assigned love language. It is somewhat like making a soup, a little of this experience — the books — and a little bit of that experience — his grandma. When it all comes together, you have one beautiful life full of the love of cooking. This leads to discovering cooking for loved ones. "That is what my grandma taught me, 'Cooking for people means love.'" I totally agree. The best way I know how to show love is to cook for people. It takes time to plan, shop, and cook. That time is worth giving to people in the form of a meal. Then sharing the food creates a common bond.

Bret shared his version of Gigi's famous recipe. Her recipe was written by hand with no specific measurements, yet lucky for us, Bret assigned the necessary specifics, and I am sharing it with you. Discover stuffed cabbage. You may just discover a little extra love.

BRET'S GRANDMA'S STUFFED CABBAGE

INGREDIENTS:
- 1 cabbage head, gently cut out core, then carefully peel off leaves one at a time, keeping them intact

FILLING:
- 2 lbs. ground beef
- 2 eggs
- 1 teaspoon salt
- 1 - 2 tablespoons onion, minced
- 2 tablespoons Matzoh meal (to bind, add more if needed)
- 1/4 cup rice, raw

SAUCE:

- 15 oz can tomato sauce
- 3 tablespoons - 1/4 cup brown sugar (less if you like less sweet, more if you like sweeter, just taste sauce and decide)
- 1 tablespoons honey
- 2 teaspoons lemon juice
- 1 tablespoons sugar
- 1/4 teaspoon salt

DIRECTIONS:

1. Starting with the cabbage leaves, put in a large pot, pour hot water over leaves and let stand in the water with a lid on for just a few minutes until the leaves start to soften. Watch them, or they will turn to mush.
2. Mix filling ingredients thoroughly together.
3. On a clean surface, lay out cabbage leaves, evenly distribute amounts of the filling in the softened leaves, and roll it up like a burrito (fold sides over filling, then roll up). How much filling depends on how many leaves you wind up with.
4. Layer evenly in a large pot.
5. Once all rolls are in the pot, pour hot water over about 1/4 of the way up the pot. Leave heat turned off.
6. In a small bowl, mix sauce ingredients besides the brown sugar together well. Then add brown sugar, starting with 3 TBS, taste, and increase until you are happy with the sweetness.
7. Pour sauce over the rolls.
8. Cover and simmer on a low flame for one hour.
9. Enjoy!

CONCLUSION

"Home is where heart is. Heart where cookie is. Math clear: home is cookie."

—COOKIE MONSTER

When I became inspired to write this book, I had no idea how thought-provoking it would be. Not just for me, but for everyone I spoke to. During my writing process, I would meet people and tell them I was writing a book to which would come the expected question, "what is it about?" As I told them, I would see the look that I have happily become familiar with—the look of reminiscing. It was beautiful, and I knew what was coming next. After a few minutes of pondering, without exception and with a smile, they would tell me the one dish that brought them back to their own childhood. With the dish, they would tell me the story. I know these individuals hadn't thought about these memories in a long time, and I happily hung on to every word. It is my true honor to be that memory catalyst.

I know now, more than ever, that what we like to eat as adults directly comes from our food experiences as children. The dishes that we return to, time and time again, in order to find comfort. After writing these stories, it is quite apparent that mothers and grandmothers played significant roles in this. So many of these remarkable stories had these same people to thank for the one dish that brought them back to their childhood.

Thank you so much for coming on this trip down memory lane with me. I truly hope you travel back to your own child-hood to rediscover the one dish that brings you back. Talk to your family. Uncover long-lost recipes. Make them! Embrace the memories. Embrace the love.

BONUS CHAPTER: LAWRY'S THE PRIME RIB

"Never eat spinach just before going on the air."

—DAN RATHER

LAWRY'S THE PRIME RIB AND THEIR FAMOUS CREAMED SPINACH

Lawry's The Prime Rib stood the test of time. According to the history section of *LawrysOnline*, their doors opened in 1938 in Beverly Hills, California. Only the prices and some new menu items have changed since the beginning. It is a restaurant that makes the past feel very much alive. The first time my Daddy took me to the famed establishment, I was probably around five. I can't count the times I've been since then. It is more than a restaurant; it's an experience.

No matter how many times I go as an adult, I become that little kid, excited and in awe of this amazing classic dining room. From the big comfortable booths that are way too close together, yet no one seems to mind, to the tables in the center of the huge dining room with big red leather chairs. The servers still wear the classic 1938 uniforms while introducing themselves as 'Ms. or Mrs. and their last name'; the chefs carve your prime rib and serve your dinner from those beautiful silver carts. As you follow your host to be seated, the inviting scent of prime rib wafts in the air and gets you excited about your pending dining experience.

Lawry's was magical to a little girl. An exciting dinner of prime rib and creamed spinach. Oh, the creamed spinach. This dish has become the one dish I look forward to over and over again. I have even learned how to make it and now share it with my family. This, to me, is pure comfort that evokes feelings of love and happiness, taking me right back to the first time I walked in the front doors and saw the palatial dining room.

I adore the history of Lawry's. So much so that I've created an episode all about it, including how to make one of the two dishes that brings me back to my childhood. This would be the creamed spinach.

For me, there are no words to describe how good Lawry's Creamed Spinach is. The cooked spinach resides in a heavenly cream sauce that has the perfect balance of salt, pepper, garlic, and my favorite thing, bacon. It's not just a side dish for me; I've had it for breakfast, lunch, and midnight snacks.

It's that good, which is why I usually triple the recipe when I make it at home.

Enjoying it at the restaurant is always my favorite. You are the audience, and the restaurant is the show—a dinner show, unlike any other, utilizing table side service. Dinner begins with Lawry's famous spinning salad bowl. A silver bowl of salad is placed in a larger bowl of crushed ice. Your server spins the bowl over the ice and, from as high as she can reach, pours their famous French dressing over the top. The spinning allows the dressing to cover the salad entirely. It's delectable.

When it is time for your main meal, the server brings with them one of the many chefs, proudly wearing a medal around their neck and white gloves to your table, politely introducing them. The chef brings with them a beautiful art-deco silver cart designed specially by the restaurant in 1938. No other restaurant has these beautiful carts or this beautiful service. They are a Lawry's original.

When the chef opens the silver cart at your table, a display of prime ribs stands alongside the traditional side dishes. You tell the server what cut and doneness you want, with your chosen sides, she tells the chef and the chef prepares your plate. The experience of sitting at your table, watching your plate being prepared, is unique. You wait in anticipation of the server putting your personalized dish in front of you.

About twenty years ago, on one of my visits to the restaurant, they made recipe cards available. One of the recipes on the card is for their creamed spinach. I still have that very card to this day, and I often make their spectacular creamed spinach from it. But not too often—it comes with many calories.

The memories of Lawry's bring me much bliss. Just writing about it transports me back to my childhood which was the beginning of my lifelong love of this restaurant. It still brings me so much happiness and comfort today.

I present dish number two, which I equally treasure. Your tummy will thank me—and Lawry's! You can easily double, triple or quadruple this recipe. And you will probably want to!

LAWRY'S THE PRIME RIB'S CREAMED SPINACH

INGREDIENTS:

- 2 packages (10 oz) chopped, frozen spinach (thawed & drained well)
- 6 slices of bacon, finely chopped
- 1/2 cup onion, chopped
- 2 tablespoons flour
- 1 teaspoon seasoned salt (I use Lawry's)
- 1 teaspoon pepper
- 2 teaspoons garlic, chopped
- 1 cup whole milk
- 1 cup half & half

DIRECTIONS:

1. Fry the bacon in a saucepan over medium heat until cooked through (not crispy). Do not drain.

2. Add to the bacon the onion, cooking until tender. Next, add garlic; cook about 2 minutes more.
3. Remove from heat, add flour, salt, and pepper. Blend thoroughly.
4. Add both milks and mix well.
5. Return to medium heat. Add spinach, breaking it up into cream sauce.
6. Cook 3–4 minutes until heated thoroughly.
7. Enjoy!

ACKNOWLEDGEMENT

This book would never have happened without the support of so many outstanding people. My gratitude for every single one of you is monumental. This has been quite the journey. I wanted to give up so many times. But there were many people I didn't want to let down, including myself. So, without further ado, my undying gratitude goes to everyone who lent a hand in my publishing journey.

First and foremost, thank you to my best friend and hubby, Rod Hecker, who gave me the gift of realizing my dreams. You were there with love and hugs through my many tears, trials, and tribulations. I could not be more grateful to you for not letting me quit when I wanted to many times. Thank you for your understanding of me being routinely absent for almost a year. I am back to enjoying retirement with you, and there is no one I would rather spend my life with.

To my Daddy, Sheldon Weinberger, for lovingly showing me the world of food and inspiring me to be who I am. I wish you were here to read this book. You would love it and my beloved YesterKitchen channel. I know you would be proud of your "sweetheart."

To Kim, Tawanna, Ian, Eric, Rick, Rod, Cindy (in Heaven), Charlene, Jason, Vanessa, Margaret, Patrick, Max, Ashley, Jimmy, Frenchy, Karen, Ilana, Alexis, Sharla, Mike, and Bret— who bravely allowed me to interview them for this memoir not knowing how their story would turn out. Thank you for your trust in me. Without you, there would be no book. My appreciation is endless for kindly putting up with my many follow-up emails. I'm especially thankful for your willingness to share a piece of your family history.

To my family and friends, too numerous to name—your love and support are unmatched, and there is no way I could have been on this journey without you. You are truly my support system. I was happily overwhelmed by all the encouragement and praise that came my way. I am unbelievably privileged to have every single one of you in my life.

To Professor Koester of Georgetown University, for teaching me that it is possible to write a book. Your care and guidance on how to write are incomparable. It is an honor to have my book in your collection.

To my entire publishing team at New Degree Press. Who knew there were so many wonderful people that went into writing a book! Your support and caring know no bounds. A special thank you goes out to my Developmental Editor, Karina, who helped me in shaping the stories, and my Marketing and Revisions Editor, Bianca DaSilva, for holding my hand, talking me off the ledge multiple times, and getting me across the finish line. And, putting up with my enormous block when it came to that darn appendix!

To my YouTube audience. You were all my inspiration for this book, and I am forever grateful. Thank you for sharing so many of your childhood memories, which helped me realize that this would make a very inspiring book. You know I look forward to hearing even more of your memories. Keep them coming; they are beautiful!

And finally, thank you to everyone that preordered my book. Your support, faith, and generosity mean so much to me. Thank you for believing in me, and as promised, you are now part of this book.

Thank you from the bottom of my heart, Alan Breslauer, Alexandre Martin, Alexis Hernandez, Ashley DePas, Bani Singh, Curt and Barb Hecker, Bianca Miller, Bill Shepherd, Brian Konowal, Chip Bush, Christine Walden, Constance La Count, Corey Brass, Daniel Pearson, David Gersten, David and Jammie Sant, David and Dana Tingle, Emily Wendel, Eric Koester, *Flour, Eggs and Yeast Channel,* Garret Hecker, Harry Reahl, Heather Poort, James Chillemi, James Mavity, Lee and Jenn Wilson, Jennifer Bradley, Jessica Caraballo, John Shaikin, Shaun and Jolayne Clem, Karen Kruse, Kevin Pham, Laura Eckhardt, Laurie and Rob Olague, Lila Ginsburg, Lisa Marie Camp, Lori Wagner, Rich and Melinda Yawn, Max Miller, Michael Granillo, Michael M Shields, Michael Prell, Mike Lopez, Patricia Anderson, Patrick Carroll, Phil Blum, Rick Scot, Rick Tresler, Ron Lisell, Rose Justice, Sharla Hulsey, Stephanie Guerrero, Steven Tobler, Jim and Terrie Hecker, Todd Moistner, Warren and Carol Holden, Wendy L Holder.

APPENDIX

———

CHAPTER 1

Positive Psychology (blog). "What Is Attachment Theory? Bowlby's 4 Stages Explained." April 27, 2018. Accessed September 8, 2021. https://positivepsychology.com/?s=attachment+theory.

Simple Psychology. *Attachment Theory. Accessed August 20, 2021.* https://www.simplypsychology.org/attachment.html.

CHAPTER 5

Bethune, Meredith. "The Sweet Success of Bananas Foster Has an Unsavory Past." *Food and Wine.* September, 30 2016. https://www.npr.org/sections/thesalt/2016/09/30/493157144/the-sweet-success-of-bananas-foster-has-an-unsavory-past.

Hutcherson, Aaron. "Like it's Complicated History, Banana Pudding has Many Layers." *Food and Wine,* June 3, 2020. https://www.foodandwine.com/cooking-techniques/banana-pudding-history-recipes.

CHAPTER 7

Knotts (blog). "The History of Knott's Berry Farm." March 31, 2020. Accessed August 13, 2021. https://www.knotts.com/blog/2020/april/the-history-of-knotts-berry-farm.

CHAPTER 9

The National WWII Museum. "Rationing." Accessed January 12, 2019. https://www.nationalww2museum.org/war/articles/rationing.

CHAPTER 11

Minnesota Department of Natural Resources. *Minnesota's All-Time Record Low.* Last modified date January 18, 2019. Accessed September 28, 2021. https://www.dnr.state.mn.us/climate/journal/960202_60_below.html.

CHAPTER 13

National Today. *Bonfire Night.* Accessed October 5, 2021. https://nationaltoday.com/bonfire-night/.

Oxford Learners Dictionary. "Catherine wheel." Accessed August 1, 2021. https://www.oxfordlearnersdictionaries.com/us/definition/english/catherine-wheel.

CHAPTER 18

WebMD. "Health Benefits of Eggs." Published June 1, 2020. Reviewed by Dan Brennan M.D. on September 8, 2020. https://www.webmd.com/diet/health-benefits-eggs.

CHAPTER 19

Rootwell (blog). "Everything You Need to Know About an Amazing Root Cellar." November 15, 2016. Accessed September 30, 2021. https://www.rootwell.com/blogs/root-cellar.

CHAPTER 20

Arthur Murray Dance Center. "History." Accessed October 15, 2021. https://arthurmurray.com/history.

CHAPTER 22

Global Kitchen Travels (blog). "Strawberry Shortcake – A History Lesson and a Recipe." October 10, 2016. Accessed October 3, 2021. https://globalkitchentravels.com/strawberry-shortcake/.

National Today. *National Strawberry Shortcake Day.* Accessed October 3, 2021. https://nationaltoday.com/national-strawberry-shortcake-day/.

University of Illinois Extension. *Strawberries & More: History & Lore.* Accessed October 3, 2021. https://web.extension.illinois.edu/strawberries/history.cfm.

CHAPTER 24

Chapman, Gary. *5 Love Languages.* Chicago: Northfield Publishing, 2015.

CHAPTER 26

Lawry's Restaurants Inc.. "Our Story." Accessed June 3, 2021. https://www.lawrysonline.com/our-story/.

Printed in Great Britain
by Amazon

45264614R00126